This book bears light.

May you discover it to be
a comforting companion to you.

GETTING TO THE
HEART OF THE MATTER

Getting to the HEART of the Matter

An Instruction Manual of Short Yet Soulful Philosophies

FRANCESCA BECCARI

BROAD BOOK STUDIO

Broad Book Studio, Publisher
Copyright © 2025 by Francesca Beccari
All rights reserved.

Interior book design by Claudine Mansour Design

Gratitude goes out to Liz Kennedy whose editing and coaching skills supported the process of this manuscript.

Hardcover: 978-1-963549-27-0 | $24.99 USD
Paperback: 978-1-963549-24-9 | $18.99 USD
eBook: 978-1-963549-25-6 | $9.99 USD

Published in the United States by Broad Book Studio, an imprint of Broad Book Group, Edwardsville, IL

Library of Congress Control Number has been applied for.

*This book is dedicated to Davio,
my late husband, who freed me and
gave me the greatest gift of all,
which he did not possess—time.*

*To my children, Anthony and Tara,
who do not know how profoundly
they remain a part of my heartbeat, and to
their children, whose lights I follow.*

*To my daughter, Heidi, who could
not be a truer or more beautiful presence.*

*And, finally, to those or perhaps
to the one that found this book and read it
because it was a timely answer;
it is for you that this book came to be.*

Without exception,
mankind is charged with this challenge:

He must face his fears,
the breath of the dragon, one by one.
He must somehow walk himself
through them. Ultimately, he will realize
and extract something positive from his pain,
never to be mastered by that fear again.

The dragon will be dead.

Contents

Author's Note

I did not want to write. One morning, I awoke with a strong feeling that I should be writing a book. At the same time, I heard these exact words.

"Brainstorm after meditation and use a clustering method."

I went back to sleep. Fifteen minutes later, I was awakened by distinct words running through my mind, I could hear.

"Write down thoughts after brainstorming."

Once again, I went back to sleep. Another fifteen minutes later I was awakened again. This time I heard,

"Do one when you go away
and everywhere else."
(I was leaving on a trip that day)

I went back to sleep and was awakened five more times at fifteen-minute intervals with the following words/instructions.

"Each man for himself."
"'Book of Songs'—Exhibit gratitude
in writing."

"There are small lessons everywhere
= writing material."

"If you build a specialty, you've got
something a little different to offer."

"Smoking thin cigars."
(That one still puzzles me)

Two days later I awoke hearing the words,

"Specialty teleconstructors—Be One."
(I had no idea what a teleconstructor was)

Following these events, I felt urged to write this book and so I did.

Preface

This is a compilation of thoughts that have been recorded by me over the years. Some of these are not my own. Peppered throughout are readings from other visionaries who have greatly inspired my life.

What remains as my own work, I will call "glimpses" that have, and do, spur me on. These are the thoughts and impressions that appear unexpectedly during deep meditation, upon first awakening, or throughout the waking day. I have attempted to translate these glimpses into concise and undiluted words.

I would ask the reader to please understand that where man or God is inferred or referred to in the masculine sense, it is for printing purposes only, for how can God be contained? Any names used here for "God" must be limiting, for I can think of none that do justice.

Contemplate the fullness of meaning on each page. Take your time. Before moving on, use each "philosophy" as a living meditation. This little book is not meant just to be read, but to inspire each, to "try on" the material, live it for a while, and watch what comes to pass. Experience the healing phenomena singularly or in groups where discussion of the results is encouraged.

Now, I Would Like to Recount an Experience of My Own

As a child, I found myself striving each day to tangibly see what I was taught "God" is. I wished to be pleasing and needed to feel the depth of who I really was, and who everyone else was. While in my twenties, a longing to become a better person was developing. I desired to live with more meaning.

A good place to start, I thought, might be to begin looking deeper into others instead of lightly passing people by. As an experiment, I began by trying to put myself into others' "shoes" by imagining that I was occupying the body and circumstances of everyone I came upon. I attempted to feel what they were feeling.

At once I became the wealthy woman. I became a beggar. I was well-mannered and refined. I was condemned and wretched.

In those days, I did not know what a mantra was, but I found myself repeating all day long as I encountered others in the flesh or in my mind, "I am you. You are me. We are one."

Honestly, I can say that one of the results of this exercise was an instant swelling of empathy; the depth of which was previously unknown to me.

Profound and lasting changes began to occur. As empathy grew, my judgment of others decreased. Compassion and tolerance increased. There was a different kind of energy around me. The kind that heals.

Since then, it has been my conviction that as mankind improves the inner world of his mind, outer manifestations of that higher thinking appear around him.

I do not expect the readers to express that which is not within us. On the contrary, I ask that we call upon the original innocent desire residing in all of us to come forth once again.

The words on these pages in and of themselves are meaningless. I cannot emphasize enough that it is only through the persistent application of these words that will have rendered this book worthwhile.

It is not my intent to entertain, but to encourage my fellow travelers as we walk the long walk together. In doing so, I am recommitted. It matters not that we fail, but only that we try again and again.

I shall not be fulfilled until I have attempted to share what have been for me, life enhancing perspectives.

While employing these concepts, either one at a time or a few at once, I ask that as much as possible, be diligent in your efforts. Never rush. Remain with the concept that you are assimilating for a period of time. Work with them until they are absorbed as your own. In doing so, your lives will expand. Due to your efforts, we, as a species, will accomplish them. Such is my pledge and motivation for my work.

Since this is a first attempt at writing, I asked myself, "Where does one begin?" I am sure now that there can be only one answer: To begin anything, one must be who one is naturally. One must, each moment, live one's truth. One must ask, "Who am I?" Then be prudent in respecting whatever that is without second guessing or masochistic judgment.

Let us each undertake this search for our Selves. While on this journey, may you enjoy an implicit trust that you are **enough** being who you are.

GETTING TO THE HEART OF THE MATTER

Who Am I?

It is believed that food sustains life, that man cannot live without water and oxygen. Why, then, if we feed a corpse food, water, and oxygen, will it remain lifeless?

It is that difference between a corpse and a living human form that is our identity.

A – B = Z
A = live body
B = corpse
_____

Z = WHO WE ARE

We are aliens who have adorned ourselves with temporary space suits called "bodies." These suits are invaluable in assisting us to function normally on Space Station Planet Earth. We are aliens. We are not our space suits. How often is there a failing to remember this as we get caught up in the daily workings of the planet? Forgetfulness cannot alter the fact that at the end of an allotted span, each of us shall lay his suit down and shall go on.

It amazes me every day to realize that creativity and uniqueness are unending and limitless. Each human, being a portion of God, just waiting for expression. Once a soul truly realizes his oneness with his Creator, he becomes a channel of limitless possibilities.

Someday Soon . . .

In a darkened room, sit in front of a mirror and light a candle for yourself. Place the candle between you and the mirror. Then relax the body and look deeply into your own eyes for a while.

What you find there may surprise you.

Remember, the eyes are the windows to the soul.

———— ✳ ————

HUMAN BEING,
you are a divine light,
a courageous portion of God

BEING HUMAN
for a short while . . .

Near death experiences are relayed by some of those who have clinically died, then returned to their physical bodies, carrying with them information from another side of life. Having listened to many accounts of those who have had near death experiences, one of the themes that frequently comes forth, is that there is no one on the other side judging us. Instead, we are shown how the actions that we took in the most recent lifetime affected others. Did I act hurtfully? How? When? To whom? I feel that too, now. Have I also affected others compassionately? How did I do that? When? To whom? I feel that now. Also, it is my own empathy for what I have done that has become my judgment and also my savior. There are no outside rules or commandments to measure oneself by.

If I were to be the recipient instead of the sender of all that I have acted upon or thought about others, how would I feel as the receiver of my thoughts, intentions and deeds?

Who is Family?

Sometimes, it shocks us to learn that our bloodline family has let us down and caused distance and emotional alienation that we never predicted. But, that shock catapults us so that we see anew, many times looking into the eyes of another kind of family, the soul connections that make up, truly, our sacred co-parts. Blood does not make a family, allegiance and dedication to one another do.

Let us be cognizant of the power, the enormity, the peace, the firefly/fire blast of love that sustains each of us and then let us address one another from that perspective which perpetually burns beyond the flesh.

It is interesting that when we allow ourselves to be who we are many times, most times, it drives others away. Even our own parents, our immediate fellows, who we are born trusting. When we shine, they shrink away, and we are seen as outsiders and left desolate. We are told, "How dare you?""Don't forget that you are lowly." We are not assisted but made to pick ourselves up and stumble to our feet and take the next step alone, and then the next step and the next, until Lo! We have become strong by negligence and others pounding on us. All of a sudden, we come to realize that the hardships and estrangements were, in fact, blessings to hone us, to begin to whittle us into the great sculptures that we are.

How sublime is the Universe, the Highest Power? Are we not born part of that sublime essence? Are we not created with the intention to go forth and shine and become new, great and fresh versions of Creation? Who are we not to? Created to be Creators. To feign our greatness is complete disregard for our soul's heritage, for the plan that birthed us into this lifetime on earth. Hiding our Light and being dim and small, backtracks not only us, but holds back those on Earth who also came to join and work with us.

Yet, there are those who demean us, placing shame on us and guilt for expressing our own beauty and vigor and talent and abilities. They purposely break our will to excel, segregating us as haughty show off braggarts, wanting attention. We have been pushed into fearing our own greatness. Rise up, fellows! See through and past. Go forth knowing that you are born of majesty and that nothing less will ever be shown by you.

When one knows himself
and his part in the larger scheme of things,
his compass is set.

He is well educated through wisdom
and can travel with little
waste of time and few detours.

Why Am I Here?

Once we begin to realize that we are not singular drops in the ocean of humanity, but that the ocean is contained within us, then we will begin to willfully move life as we are meant to.

Two observations to contemplate:

1. There is something to be learned and experienced by imagining oneself as a drop in the vastness of the ocean, allowing

existence to place us where it will and "going with the flow," without resistance. Relax and take some time to let this thought sink in until you feel the reality of it.

2. Another practical form of constructing the future is to get comfortable and silent. Then, imagine that not only the whole ocean, but the planet, the galaxy and beyond, be contained within you.

Do you feel the difference? Now, create with your emotions, the most ideal state imaginable within our Milky Way galaxy home. Stay until the feelings are full within you.

We have the ability yea, the responsibility to affect Life. May those intentions be of the highest imaginable!

Ever wonder if you are finished with your life's mission? Our Higher Selves know when and how we can be most beneficial to Creation. Be sure that if you are currently living on Earth, then there is still more to learn and teach before transitioning to another dimension. You are still useful as you do your job and live your everyday life. In other words, it is not your time to cross over yet.

Imagine that you have one week left to live on Earth.

Now, ask yourself the following questions:

+ Is there a single, pressing thing that I have left undone?

+ What is it that I feel I simply must do or say before l leave?

+ Who will I spend my remaining precious moments with?

The answers to these questions are related to your life's purpose here and the reason you were born.

At the end of physical life, who will abide with you into the abyss of eternity? Can those of the Earth help you then? When you judge yourself, what will matter, that you found worldly acclaim or divine acclaim? In all things, seek not recognition from man. Instead, seek recognition from your conscience.

If you are still living on planet Earth, then your mission is not yet finished.

Strive to graduate from Earth School with honors.

What will it take?

The most gratifying of life's work is engaging in labor that is honest, pure, motivating and comes naturally to the doer. When unsure of which way to go, simply ask, "Do I feel more comfortable taking this action, or am I more comfortable taking that action? Which feels better in my belly? Saying this or saying that? Right or left? Is 'yes' more settling in my being, or is 'no'?" It is unnecessary to know the outcome of our choice of which way to go or what to choose, because our souls are always urging us in the direction of most growth and what is most appropriate and best. Always act on the feelings that are most deeply comforting in the moment. You do not have to know where the outcome is, only that at this moment, you are doing what feels the least intrusive to your being, knowing that this choice will make your conscience feel the softest.

You will know very soon if you have not chosen your higher path because if a better way has become available, feelings of discomfort will arise in you. How do you know what your personal work is? What is your heart telling you? What feels right within your conscience?

ACT on it!

When one walks into a completely dark room and shuts the door, one is in total darkness. Now, if one then lights a little, tiny candle, one is no longer in darkness. What lives and has been thriving in the dark can no longer survive in an environment of luminosity and must either escape or perish. The light of who we are exposes and expels dark spirits. Never underestimate the power of your light as you move through the world. Know that by your compassionate intentions alone, are you a lamp unto the Universe.

You are.

———— ✳ ————

We are notes in the ongoing composition of time. Are we prepared to hear the music we make? Is it shrill? Is it tender? As we manifest our innate gifts, we come to realize that in some way, we are unique. If we are gracious enough with ourselves, we will continue to develop our gifts.

Should everyone simultaneously, and to the

best of their ability, utilize their own talent, we would as a race of individual people, be in such exquisite harmony. Only then will we create on this massive rock, Mother Earth from which we suckle, an unprecedented masterpiece not unlike the heavenly music of dreams.

When we are truly ourselves, we become at once not only the notes of the living master-piece, but the composer and the composition.

How Much Have I Loved?

It seems that at the end of
one's life as we know it, the
answer to this question shall be
the only one that matters. The
answer to this question is why
we awaken each day. It is
everything. Nothing else but
love can be taken with us when
we leave.

Love is the eternal luminary
that other souls may find us and
we, them.

On Romantic Relationships

Some years ago, a romantic involvement was causing me considerable distress. Longing to diffuse and resolve the pain, I fervently asked for understanding. I found myself mentally crying out, "Teach me about relationships!" Not long after, while sitting alone one evening in that land somewhere between sleeping and waking consciousness, the following vision appeared: I am in a vast space. The darkness is punctuated by beings who seem to be shimmering, pulsating, somewhat round spheres of light. Each is distinguished by the unmistakably unique shades and patterns that it consists of. One of these beings is me. In awe, yet surprisingly serene, I watch as two of these merges to become one light body. After time, there is a parting and while they are separate once again, there is a difference about them. They seem to have become more, because each has taken on a bit of the other's color and brilliance.

These two who were once a unit have parted. Still watching, I am succinctly aware that the whole event is absolutely void of negativity. There is no pain, regret, no fear experienced by either being. These two "light spheres" are now heading in different directions. One seems to be flying, one floating among the other billions like them. With great joy, they explore separately until once again, each join with a new being. As before, they part, and now each exists individually as the sum of its own innate beauty, the beauty of the light sphere it had joined with previously, and now supplemented by the qualities of the new partner. Through all of this, each seems to be moving to its own rhythm and timing, yet harmony presides like a square-dance without form. This behavior continues. It is the way of life. One at a time, through this process, they are becoming increasingly diverse and intricate yet remain uniquely distinct. I am struck by the absence of jealousy.

> *All seem to know that there is an abundance of experiences to be had with as many as one wish to unite with. Emotions of loss or separation are nonexistent here. Instead, there is immense contentment in knowing that forever, each shall inhabit a portion of the beauty and color of those who have touched them. And each shall take delight in having left behind a degree of loveliness to adorn all with whom they have danced. Such was my vision, my lesson.*

Could boredom endure if we live as if each experience were new to us?

+ It doesn't matter how much time you have spent with someone. Look at that person in a new light. Focus your attention on a different quality within him than you normally would. Experience him as if for the first time with no comparisons to the past.

+ The next time you are eating a meal, taste it as if you never had it before. Savor your food with new expectations.

+ On your way home or on some other familiar route, stop for a moment. Though you may have passed that way hundreds of times, pause to take in the wonder of nature. Feel it. Let it touch you in a way that it never has. Just be there as if the whole world were new to you.

Apply this technique often. Use it at work and during your leisure hours. Use it on everyone, everything, everywhere. It is a mighty tool that will empower and refresh your relationships.

You will discover attributes and nuances that you've never noticed but were always there. Your life and the lives around you will become enriched and you will be more interesting—especially to yourself.

When giving birth to our sensuality, our children and our myriad businesses still leaves us barren, perhaps then, we will venture inward and strive to realize the fulfillment of a new kind of birth—the birth of our finer selves.

When the yearning to have children is non-existent, it's time to recreate oneself. This is done by harnessing the fire of the sex glands through control, balance and mastering our sexual energy. In so doing we then are fueling our love, intuition and genius to better serve.

Sex and Relationships

I've yet to meet a person who isn't enthralled with the intoxication of new love. A fresh feeling of love is another aspect of our deeper yearning for Divine Love. Is it possible to be with others we've known a long time or to be by oneself, yet feel the kind of bliss that one experiences when he has just fallen in love? How can we carry this kind of love with us each minute? Perhaps the oneness, the feeling that another has become a part of us, or we are a part of them, can be explored with other objects that are around us. In other words, emotionally, we can make love to anything. Expand the attention and lovemaking attitudes toward all things and wait for the response. It will be there. The desire to share and listen and become one will be the initiation. That desire will be the beginning of a life lived in the Divine expression. Look no longer toward only humans to give that temporary "head over heels" feeling of love. Go within. Look to all things. Know the oneness. Make Love. First to yourself, and then all around you.

Think about this—our bodies have the ability to produce other human beings. Expelling our orgasms holds within it, creation itself!

Now that I have had my children, I think about continuing to use my sexual energy, not to have more babies, but to keep that fire energy inside of me for a different type of creation. I wish to re-create myself. The power of my sex energy kept within, pushes toward new potential, new strength, stamina. Its' tributaries can be felt in the heightening of one's unique gifts. For instance, artwork becomes more artistic, conversations more succinct, the healing energies more powerful, etc. Choosing to master and hold those sexy energies in, will cause one to vibrate at a higher frequency. You will feel so magnetic, creative, sexier than if you had allowed your body to spill with orgasm. Awareness will become sharper, and you will feel more alive, but at a higher level.

When the time is ripe and one longs to produce a finer self instead of reproducing another human, refrain from orgasm. That does not mean that one must refrain from sex. It means control. Lots of it!

I have found that if a couple wishes to bring their relationship to new levels of closeness, they should practice methods of enjoying sex with each other, but both partners stopping before climax. They will become extremely magnetic to one another, constantly seeking each other and driven to enjoy the pleasure of lovemaking. Because there is no climax, they become an unfinished symphony. Do not underestimate the power in your sex glands. They have produced your children. What will they produce in you, should you decide to control and master your sex drive?

Feeling bored? Want to refresh a marriage? Are you wishing to enjoy more excitement within your existing relationships? Here is an anecdote: See things as if for the first time, and without any memories of them whatsoever. When you encounter your loved ones, gaze upon them as if you are seeing them for the first time. Erase all past knowledge, perceptions or any known traits about them. Banish all of that from your mind. Imagine that this is the first time that you are coming upon them. Then, say to yourself, "Without any history, who is this person that I am now looking at?" See him or her in a fresh light. Look with attention until you begin to observe things that you've never noticed before. A new appreciation will arise within you.

Don't forget the relationship that you have with yourself, which is constantly evolving. At any given moment, ask yourself, "Without history, who am I in this moment? If this is my first day on the planet with no prior experiences or relationships, who am I and what do I want?" Listen and feel for the answers. Begin to act on the new layer of yourself that you've just acknowledged. You will not be bored.

Listening

When I am crushed with hardship When I cannot take even another step, I shall stop:

Heart! Oh heart!
In the mysterious language that is yours, reveal
to me the hidden meaning of these circum-
stances!

What am I to learn here?

What am I to teach?

When my mind cries out against over-whelming difficulties, let my heart show me the underlying lesson.

As I listen, I shall hear.

Reflections on Meditation

What am I without the daily touch and feel of home? How do I go with such numbness of neglect? How feeble, time wasting, energy dissipating are my actions when taken before meeting with the great Encompassor. It is that ever sweet ethereal touch, the contact made that sweetens my moments into the day. It is that ride through the only umbilical cord of true survival that nurtures and sustains, which gives all providing fulfillment. It is the peace that guides, leads, illumines, hints, teaches and gives a sense of, "I just feel that this is the right thing to do now."

So much smoother is our sojourn here when we make time to hear the promptings that occur during deep listening. Such is our compass, our navigator, and all that keeps us from becoming lost. Let us be aware of and enter into this inside place often, that we may inherit the riches of tranquility and clear moments of insight that await. May we experience the joy of receiving Cosmic hugs. All of us know when we are getting one. The heart feels bigger. Our generosity expands. We have an excess to give because we are full without direction, without daily contact, without the ebb of taking in and the flow of gratitude, are our actions worth our while? Brothers and sisters, meditate! Loved ones, persevere! Persevere.

No Longer Making Mistakes

I have learned to eliminate a good amount of daily stress by no longer second guessing myself, but acting instead, on the first impulse that I feel. Whatever is tugging at me or giving me a sense of which way is more comfortable in that moment is where I direct my attention and energy.

For instance, each day, before my feet touch the floor, I acknowledge that I am never alone.

I ask my invisible Helpers to guide and accompany me in all my doings of the day, to lead me, and to speak through my words. Once I remember that I am indeed working within a team of the highest caliber, I am then certain that no matter what happens, because my Helpers are always involved, that everything will always be working out for the best for me.

Should you wish to live in this manner, past expectations must be dropped to make way for the new, fresh "whispers" of inspiration and ways of doing things that will be more relevant and effective than the ways of the past. It means not feeling guilty when you thought you should have done something that did not get done. Here is an example of how I experience less stress in daily living: One day I packed a bag of food into my car, planning to bring it to the local food bank during the day between completing errands. When I arrived home at the end of the day, the bag containing food was still in my car. I had not thought to drop it off. In prior days, I would have chastised myself for being forgetful and felt somewhat disappointed in myself. But, as I am living now, I instead remind myself that I am never alone and that everything is always working out for the best for me. If the highest action that I could have taken during that day was to have the food delivered, I would have remembered to go. I would have been nudged as a reminder to go. But, since the thought did not cross my mind, that was acknowledgment to me that I cannot see the whole picture of life and that I correctly followed my instincts, remembering that "Everything is always working out for the best for me." Another day began to turn into evening as I drove a bag of food to the food bank. When I arrived, it was closed, but an old pickup truck sat in the driveway. A young boy of about fourteen was outside in the back of the truck. His mother was in the driver's seat. It was obvious that they were hungry, and the boy looked embarrassed. Trying to be stealthy, I pretended not to see them and placed the bag where they could easily get it, then scurried back to my car. As I drove away, the woman shouted, "I am so glad that you came!" I yelled back, "I'm so glad you're here!"

What a lovely moment that was, a lesson

showing me what happens when we trust and allow life to unfold for the day; to stop judging ourselves after we follow our inner instincts and intuition. Once we've asked for guidance and we have decided to honor it by listening, feeling minute to minute which way to go and what to do or say, we can trust that no more mistakes will be made. We will know that everything is always working out for the best when our Higher Being is navigating.

Do You Face a Major Decision? Are You Indecisive?

Find a quiet, comfortable spot where you won't be interrupted:

- Now, close your eyes and imagine yourself floating.

- Allow yourself to gently float higher and higher until you can see the whole Earth below you.

- Think about your life's commitment to the planet and to humanity.

- Now, from this perspective, ask yourself, "Will the result of the decision I am about to make promote love, cohesiveness and growth?"

If so, and if there is sincerity, you are making a beneficial decision.

Mental dialogue is so one sided! How often do you cease the mind's chatter and sink into silence?

Be a good listener during meditation. It's not polite to talk all of the time.

Don't disappoint the Universe when it tries to get a point across.

Deeper Education

The term "higher education" is not limited to only scholarly studies but includes another type of learning. There are things one cannot learn outside of one's self. Lessons of the soul taught in silence; that glimmer, that ray of knowing that strikes one in peaceful repose. Gradually becoming aware of this (oh so gently given) knowledge is a portion of what comes to mind when I hear the term "higher education." Perhaps a better term would be "deeper education."

*"Everything is always
working out for the best for me."*

Before your feet hit the floor each morning, give permission to allow assistance into your day and life. Know that everything you will do today is being done with the accompaniment of your spiritual team. Once you have asked for and acknowledged that you will not be alone, that you will be helped in all that you do, all that you say and all that you experience, then trust. Feel the comfort of safety, knowing that, **"Whatever happens to me, I am aware that I cannot see the whole picture. I know that the oversight of my team is experiencing along with me. I remind myself all day long, that although I may not understand why, everything is always working out for the best for me."** Memorize and say this during the day, but only with conviction. **"Everything is always working out for the best for me."** This statement will be true for you when you truly believe it.

Once upon a time, I was very much in love with a man. I thought we belonged to each other. When he left me for that nurse, oh! How I writhed with longing and agony. I would scream to myself, "Why? Why?" About a month later, he had an accident and became incontinent and paralyzed from the waist, down, completely dependent. I saw that nurse of his taking care of him. Could I have done what she was doing? Would I have wanted to?

Everything is always working out for the best for me.

"Be Here Now."
What Does This Mean?

Being—To BE. To be in the present. This means focusing one's attention fully on what is at hand—without a past—having a vision of the future, but not worried about it. Really experiencing the sights, the smells, the feelings, the sensations, really listening.

Life will immediately become richer as we learn to move deeper into each moment.

Who Are You?
Where Have You Come From?
Where Are You Going?

Surely, the answers to these are deserving of a lifetime of consideration. As for me, they are the ultimate questions.

Now and then, it might be insightful to consider these questions in the following manner.

Recite one sentence at a time. Each time

the thought is repeated, emphasize a different word.

For example:
WHO Am I?
Who **AM** I?
Who Am **I**?

Before meditating, I asked myself intently: Why am I without direct guidance in my life? Where am I to go? What do I do next?

Later, in meditation, I sense this message: "Clean up your act! Raise your energy to a higher vibration so that you can 'hear.'"

To me, this translates into something like this: "Act on what you know to do now that would make your conscience feel clean. It's not enough to know what to do. It is not enough to aspire. DO what you know. Then you will have cleared out some of the gross noise and debris. Now the finer stuff can be heard or known.

Thy Will Be Done vs. My Will Be Done

By taking time each day for prayer (which is active supplication), and meditation (which is passive listening), we begin to think like the gods that we are. We begin to desire the highest outcomes for ourselves and others. Our minds become tuned to loftier ideals.

Our own willpower becomes fueled with the divine power that is the result of daily meditation. We become our higher selves as we merge with that still, small voice within. Our thoughts are then accompanied by a benevolent force.

Then we can truly say, "Thy will be done," and know that thy and I are one and the same will.

During quiet times of reflection, I had been wholeheartedly expressing one of my sincere desires. I wanted to clearly recognize any communication coming to me from a higher perspective. Some would call it the Higher Self. A short time later, I had the following dream:

My mailman is annoyed because I have three mailboxes instead of one. He has a difficult time getting into them. The mailboxes have to be cleaned and the openings where the mail is dropped have to be made larger. The mailman feels that one big clean mailbox would solve his problems.

Let us take a closer look and study the symbolic language within the dream:

I suppose this dream is telling me that as yet, I am not an ideal receiver (mailbox). If I am to be a fit receptacle for information and guidance, it would behoove me to become less scattered and three times more focused and dedicated to this endeavor. Being more open and clearing my own mind would help make room for the communication for which I have asked.

Music

Carry us into the heart of God as we meditate on your piercing language!

If the Divine was music without words, what would it say to you?

Pretend that it is.
Now Listen.

Record your thoughts afterwards.

There is a small room in my home where I enjoy spending an hour or two each day listening to beautiful music. A comfortable chair and my favorite Afghan are in there. Evelyn made it for me.

But before entering, I try to leave all my problems and worries outside the door. They are not welcome in this room. Once the door is shut, I sit comfortably, savoring, feeling each note. I listen as if hearing music for the first time. It is at this point that my body and mind begin to take refreshment.

Make room.

Remember that you are a child of divine heritage, a part of the creation of all things, a part of the mind of God and the voice of God on Earth. Always ask in meditation, "Show me what it is that I need to know now." Remembering that, "The whisperings in your mind are God's voice." I pay deep attention, listening as I go about my day, watching for signs. I know the answers will come in a myriad of ways and in their perfect timing. When you calm down, guidance is always tiptoeing around you. You just need to turn the focus inward and ask these questions: What? How? Where? What feels the most comfortable choice in this moment? Then you know that is the way to go! Trust yourself. Each time we give in to the whisperings of our soul, we begin to learn that we can trust ourselves, every day and all day. I start by asking, "Show me." Then I relax until a feeling or a word or an urge comes to me. That is when I take my first step in the direction that feels correct, although I do not know yet the destination. I know that each moment takes care of itself.

At 25 years old, I left my marriage. We had been living in Canada, although I was a citizen of the United States. One day, I found myself walking over the Canadian Bridge into the United States, with two children, a 9-month-old and a 22-month-old. I had no car, no money, no plan, nor did I know how I would get milk and diapers or a roof over our heads when I got to the other side of the bridge. I was terrified but knew that I had to move forward. For the first time that I could remember and to my surprise, I felt words being impressed upon me. I heard, "Don't look back. Don't look back." I knew that if I did, I would panic. Then, I was given instructions intuitively. "Focus only on this hour. Do not look forward. Do not look back. Do not think about anything that might be beyond this hour. Right now, you are all safe. Just think about right now. Do not look beyond this hour." Those words were all I had to grasp onto, and I listened. Soon, I learned that focusing on only this hour in time, what I must do right now in this hour, turned into the next, and the next, until a day had passed, that day turned into a week, and then months. I learned that looking back at the past which was gone, or trying to see what might be in the unknown future was paralyzing.

On Health

Think of the person you love most. Feel the tenderness that resides between you and that other. Let it fill you. (Take as much time as you need.)

Allow those feelings to spill over and spread out to include anyone in the nearby vicinity. (Once again, take all the time you need).

Now expand your tenderness further. Set it loosen to encompass everyone everywhere.

This is the kind of activity that heals.

Our memories can make us grow old quicker.

*Forgetting is a secret that may
keep us eternally young.*

I Understand That My Body is a Mirror That Steadfastly, Faithfully, and Accurately Reflects My State of Mind and Emotions

A woman was told that she had two hernias. She went to a doctor's appointment where it was relayed to her that these hernias could be repaired, but first the doctor wanted to see exactly what they had to work with via an MRI. The scan was taken, and she left her appointment to meet a few people for a drink and something to eat.

It was early Friday evening and the conversation in the restaurant was lively when her phone rang. It was the doctor whom she had seen earlier in the day. He conveyed to her that he and others were looking at her MRI results and that they saw something they did not like. He told her to come back to the hospital that night and to speak to a specialist who showed her the inside of her body on a screen. He explained that he and other doctors who had looked at her scans concurred that she had what looked like the beginning of pancreatic cancer. He suggested an exploratory surgery be done very soon.

Upon awakening from the anesthesia after the procedure, a doctor was above her saying that they wanted to do another surgery. She asked why. He told her they wanted to take out body parts from three areas. She asked when they wanted to perform the surgery. He answered, "Yesterday."

She went home to think about it and remembered that she had read articles and seen videos about cancer cells loving to eat sugar. She also learned that cancer cells cannot live in a body that is alkaline. Baking soda alkalizes the body. Molasses is sweet. She remembered seeing doctors curing cancer by having their patients drink tea twice a day of pure water, baking soda, and molasses. Under a microscope, she watched cancer cells be destroyed after ingesting the tea.

She knew that good Rick Simpson Oil from the cannabis plant is also known to cure cancer, just by taking the size of a grain of rice twice a day. And so, she drank tea and placed a drop of the Rick Simpson oil on something sweet twice a day for about six weeks.

She hasn't gotten sick since, nor did she ever go back for a checkup. (As of this writing, many years have gone by, and she is radiantly healthy.)

Don't be afraid to take matters into your own hands.

Bodily Symptoms as Symbolic Signs of Disease

Want to know what is causing the disease, the distress? Look at the part of the body, determine what its function is, where that function is malfunctioning in your life, and then you will understand the cause of your medical problem.

The doctor told me that I had a cyst on my left ovary and should have it surgically removed. Since I was not in pain, I dismissed the

48   ✳   Francesca Beccari

diagnosis. During the next yearly examination, the doctor said that the cyst on my left ovary had disappeared, but that I then had a different cyst on my right ovary. He recommended surgery, and I asked him why I would consent to a surgery, when the first cyst dissipated on its own. He answered that what happened was a quirk, and that something like that is not going to happen again. I opted to wait, although against his prescribed surgery.

The next yearly exam showed that I had no cysts on either ovary, but I did, indeed, have a tumor the size of an orange on my uterus. The doctor insisted on surgery and promised that if I did not, I would be in a lot of pain. Once again, I opted against the surgery, so the doctor discharged me as his patient because I refused to heed his advice, saying, "When you are in enough pain, you will come back begging."

I went home, and said to myself, "Okay, what parts of my body are affected? They are the parts that have to do with my femininity, my womanhood, my sexuality."

Then I asked, "Where in my life is my femininity, womanhood or sexuality distressed or uneasy?" As soon as I asked that question, the immediate thought that came up was of the romantic relationship that I was involved in. I was feeling increasingly unappreciated while steadily giving to a partner and a relationship that was no longer nurturing or feeding my spirit. Realizing that the link between my female parts being in distress and my longing for a fulfilling romantic partnership was simultaneously distressing me, I knew exactly what I had to do.

That relationship quickly and permanently ended and so did all the female problems.

In essence, the body was accurately mirroring my feelings, and I did need surgery, but not the physical kind. I was led to sever what was bothering me in my life. Once done, the body did not need to express illness any longer.

A Road to Recovery

Ask yourself what, on your body, hurts. What part of your body is ill at ease at the moment? Then take note of the functions of the unhealthy area. What job does that portion of the body have? What does it represent? Once you have clarified the main body part that is malfunctioning or ill, and you know what its general purpose is, you have accomplished the initial step toward healing. Now:

+ Ask yourself, "Where in my life am I not peaceful?" Correlate where you are distressed in your everyday life and thoughts, to the body part that is also distressed. For example, if you have a toothache, you know that teeth chew and bite.

+ Then correlate in your life, what you have been "chewing" on, but have not spit out. Is there something that needs to be spoken but hasn't? Or possibly words have been spoken by you that were "biting." Another example might be realizing how back pain could be caused by feeling that one is "carrying a heavy load" financially, emotionally, etc. Having hearing loss? What is it you don't wish to hear? Vision blurry? What do you not want to see? These are generalizations, but you get the idea. You have now completed the second step of your healing process.

+ Lastly, you must now change the course of things in your life to rectify what it is that's ailing you. Make modifications in your circumstances. If you cannot alter the circumstances, then decide to change the way you FEEL about what is bothering you. Make a decision to internalize the problem in a different way or not at all. Deep honesty, taking responsibility and an unflinching vision of yourself as healthy and having overcome is essential. Do these things and you will heal on many levels.

There are hundreds of ways to reduce stress. Some have found the following method helpful:

+ Just rest your body and imagine yourself as a hollow bamboo stem. Feel that you are newly born and empty inside. If thoughts begin to fill your mind, gently let them go, and focus once again on how new, empty and clear you are.

+ For some, lovely music playing in the background can be conducive to relaxation. For others, the sounds of nature can be calming. Still, there are those who prefer listening to the silence of their own mind when it is unruffled by shivering thoughts.

Fear Is a Strong Emotion

I understand that my body is a mirror that steadfastly, faithfully, and accurately reflects my state of mind and emotions.

I don't know whether we will ever discover THE fountain of youth. Should we ever come upon it, though, I suspect that the love in our eyes, the kind word on our lips, the abiding optimism in our chest, and the ability to repeatedly forgive would have been some of our guideposts.

I refuse to expect old age to accompany my body with disease. Instead, I turn within and allow myself to be showered daily through meditation which is my medication. My health is my choice and my command.

Let us remember that the feelings, emotions and beliefs that we hold for a repeated amount of time will magnetize toward us as additional circumstances that will cause us to experience increased amounts of the same feelings, emotions and beliefs, whether they are pleasant or not. When we do anything because we are afraid of what will happen if we don't . . . that is detrimental and harmful to us. Are we eating well because we're afraid of what might happen if we don't? Are we praying out of fear? Do we exercise because we are afraid, or because we love to? Strong underlying feelings of fear can be more powerful than our conscious good deeds and intentions. It would do us well to examine which side of the scale we live on. It is fear, not food, that kills us.

If you do not want your disease to return.
Take heed that you have
changed the thoughts, emotions, and deeds
that brought on the sickness.

Why Chronic?
Body Follows the Mind

Someone was constantly complaining about a medical problem. She was given a remedy, which helped for a short while, but then the malady returned. She was given a different remedy, that others had used with great success in healing and ridding themselves of the illness, but she was not cured. Other new remedies were given and each time, she was either helped for a short while before her sick symptoms recurred, or she wasn't helped in the least. She would whine that, "Nothing works for me," and become argumentative when someone would suggest that the problem can be overcome.

Then, one day I finally understood why she was having this chronic problem. She had a mindset of being sickly. In everyday conversations, she would often say things like, "Oh, I can't go there because of my disease." Or "My (such and such disease) causes me to feel sleepy." It is impossible for a body to heal when the mind has no intention of health. She owned her illness, and so it was hers.

*The diploma of soul expansion is
the reward for experiencing change.*

*Delaying graduation by refusing to
make appropriate changes can make us ill.*

We are matriculated.

Sun Gazing

A beloved child was having a difficult time seeing the things that her teacher wanted the students to look at in the classroom. Each time she went to her eye doctor's appointment, she came away with a stronger eyeglass prescription, and thicker glasses. Watching that time after time, I wondered if there were other ways that I didn't know about to improve eyesight.

I found the work of a man named Hira Ratan Manek, who was sometimes referred to as HRM. He was looking at the full round ball circumference of the sun and began to speak about his findings, professing the many advantages of doing so. Of the benefits he claimed, improved eyesight was one of them. My curiosity was hopefully aroused.

Basically, his theory was that without sunlight, there is no food, therefore, food is a byproduct of the sun's energy. Humans have been indirectly getting sun energy by eating, although there is less of the sun's energy available in meat than there is in fruit and produce.

Manek taught that we could get our nourishment straight from the sun more effectively by slowly and gently allowing sunlight to directly enter the body through the eyes, eventually lighting upon the brain, resulting in better functioning human beings. That is why, he explained, appetite is reduced when sun gazing time increases, because the body no longer needs as much sunlight normally taken in from food once pure sunlight is being absorbed through the eyes.

I set out to try his process firsthand so that I could know truly if doing so would be beneficial. Following his instructions, I learned that it was safe to look at the sun during the first hour of sunrise and during the last hour before sunset while the sun was still completely round.

This must always be done naturally without wearing eyeglasses or contacts. He taught that one who wishes to begin this method should begin the first day by looking into the sun for only 10 seconds. The second day, watch the sun for 20 seconds, adding 10 seconds each day building up to 45 minutes.

Once I began the sun gazing process, subtle changes started to occur. The first thing I noticed was that my intuition became more prominent. The aches in my joints disappeared and my happiness quotient went up. I noticed that if I missed a day because of cloudiness or rain in the sky, my mood was not as peaceful and I was less hungry. Previous physical ailments disappeared, and my vision actually improved.

As time went on and my sun gazing times increased, I noticed that my dream life, which was always prolific, had begun to subside. It seemed that the longer my sun watching times was, the less my dreams impacted me.

Since dreams come to guide, counsel and show the way, and since my intuition was increasing due to watching the sun, perhaps there was less needed to dream at night because my intuition was guiding, counseling and showing me the way during waking hours. I do continue to dream at this time, though less bountifully.

All the above has been and continues to be an ongoing personal experiment for me. Manek taught that once people reach the 45-minute mark of sun watching, it was time for maintenance. He said that practitioners should begin walking barefoot on sand or thick soil for 45 minutes every day with the sun hitting the top of their heads and look at the sun at sunrise or sunset for 15 minutes 3 times a week.

That was Manek's tutelage, and I decided to test out my personal inklings and went past the 45-minute mark. I wanted to know what the effects would be on me personally, since I was feeling so wonderful, and my vision had sharpened as if I was watching high-definition TV.

Each day I looked at the sun, adding 10 more seconds, until I reached a solid maximum of 4 hours and 46 minutes of straight gazing into the sun. Of course, that took me out of the one hour after sunrise or one hour before sunset parameter that I had kept to earlier.

By that time, there seemed to be a lot of

what I will call energy around me. Mechanical things were breaking down in my home. I went through three refrigerators within a five-year period. My car was faulting, the oven stopped heating, washing machine and dryer had problems, technology did strange things, etc. One day as I walked into the laundry room, a night light that was securely plugged into the wall, flew out of its' socket and landed across the room, breaking the glass light bulb.

That was my sign that it was time to make some changes. I stopped sun gazing all together for a few months and noticed that things stopped malfunctioning around the house. That was good. In contrast, though, my vision lost its' high-definition quality which I enjoyed so much, and at times I started to feel twinges of achiness in certain joints.

So, I started looking at the sun again for 45 minutes at a time about three times a week, but I never did the barefoot walking that Manek advised. During that time, in the year 2023, it felt as if the effects of the sun were changing somehow, or I was experiencing the sun in a different way. Presently, as I watch 2024, I am being urged to proceed at fifteen minutes a day, and seem to get more benefit closer to midday, when the sun is closest to the Earth.

This is an ongoing, evolving experiment for me, which changes over time. As of this writing, I have begun to be "told" when to prepare to go out and look at the sun. Yes, I hear songs and word lyrics in my mind telling me to do so, but each person's knowing, and intuition works differently.

As of late, in an occasional dream or heartfelt message, I have been advised to look at the moon. Unsure as to what phase of the moon or what time of evening is best, I am sure that the way will show itself, as it does for all of us in time. Let us see how this unfolds, and what is next, shall we?

Unhappiness to Joy

Happiness is a state of mind one chooses. No one can make you happy but yourself; nor can anyone take that happiness away from you. No one.

You do not have to take the bad with the good. Instead, accept only the good onto your being and only the good will magnetize to you.

Stare only at what you want. Through a lens of love, stare.

When I finally learn to cease causing pain not only to others, but to myself; when my first reaction is to find love everywhere and in everything, then all my living will have been worthwhile.

Leave no kind thought unexpressed.

The more that you can do without, the more fearless you will be.

Many who find themselves depressed and unhappy wish and pray for their circumstances to change for the better. Though changes may come, happiness is not guaranteed. True joy is the result of inner transformation. Joy is the prize for a mind that chooses to dwell daily, in every situation, on the highest qualities of life. For those who seek first to enrich their inner life, lasting improvement of the outer life is certain.

A True Test in Forgiveness

Quietly think of someone dear to you. From the center of your heart, radiate your warm, loving feelings to that person. Stay with this awhile.

Now radiate the same compassion in the same measure to someone who has hurt you.

Hint: This is not work. This is an unburdening of a load that you have been carrying.

Lessons Learned in Poverty

The less we must maintain, the freer we are to discover, examine and then express more of the Divine attributes that is our essence.

Some of the happiest moments in my life, when I was bursting and purposeful and driven, were times when the sheer love I focused on another, held that human being, up. I learned that the power of just one soul loving me truly, is a bridge to anywhere I dare to go. This knowledge is not earned from having money.

There was a homeless man who did not have a place to call home. He lived on the streets and often walked my neighborhood. When I tried to give alms, he refused it, telling me that he used to be a prominent businessman, and that he had become a slave of his own making with too much pressure and stress and now, he is free and much happier.

When one is in poverty and desolation without a vision, there is nowhere else to turn, but within. It takes deep faith to trust one's guidance. That is where true and lasting lessons are learned.

Do not live extraneously, or in a way that would compare to others' lives. Live as simply as possible while maintaining a comfortable life. The less we must maintain, the freer we are to discover, examine and then express more of the Divine attributes that are our essence. When there is no material thing left to give, give of your soul riches where you are eternally wealthy.

Promise yourself to be so strong that nothing can disturb your peace of mind.

+ To talk health, happiness and prosperity to every person you meet.

+ To make all of your friends feel that there is something exceptional in them.

+ To look at the sunny side of everything and make your optimism come true.

+ To think only of the best, to work only with the best of your ability and expect only the best.

- To be just as enthusiastic about the success of others as you are about your own.

- To forget the mistakes of the past and press on to the greater achievements of the future.

- To wear a cheerful countenance at all times and give every living creature you meet a smile.

- To give so much time to the improvement of yourself that you have no time to criticize others.

Move Out of Your Way

Many years ago, during a busy Saturday morning in a beauty shop, I was drying the hair of a customer. Another hairdresser's customer, who frequented the salon every Saturday, came in complaining of back pain. She took a seat, and her operator applied bleach to her hair, then set a timer to alert her when it would be time to wash her hair.

While she waited for the bleach to do its' job, I kept being drawn to notice that she was encountering more and more pain. Finally, she jerked up, and loudly said, "Get this off of my head! I cannot take this pain any longer." She made her way to the sink, although her hair color had not yet finished its' job, sat down and asked the shampoo assistant to cleanse her hair, then call an ambulance for her.

I was still working on drying the person's hair in front of me. Something inside of me was pushing me to go over to the woman in pain, but I thought to myself, "What would I do when I get there?", so I did not. Instead, I kept working, while the urge inside of me kept getting stronger. Again, I tried to ignore the pull I was feeling and once again thought, "But what could I possibly do when I get there?" Trying to disregard the inclination to go over to the woman, I kept working.

Suddenly, my hands began to shake so that I could no longer hold the blow dryer that I was using. Finally, I turned off the dryer and went to her in the middle of her shampoo. I said, "I don't know why I am doing this, but I feel as if I should touch your head. Would you mind?" The shampoo assistant stepped aside. The woman was open and welcoming as I placed my hands upon her head for several moments. No words were spoken. With calm and steady hands, I went back to my customer, and the shampoo assistant finished rinsing the woman's hair. When the woman left the sink area, she instructed the assistant to cancel the ambulance.

The next day I received a call from the woman, saying that she was without pain, and asking what I did to her. I said to her that whatever happened came through me, not from me. I just allowed it to flow.

Think of the soul that you most revere, whether in the flesh or not. Have you forgotten that you are also a part of the same essence of that one that you hold in high regard? The same spark of light that enlivens your chosen one, also exists within you. What you do with this power is up to you. Everyone in every moment has the choice to act like a common follower, an animal in a herd of cattle, or to allow the guard to drop and act out the powerful creators that we are. Mediocre or majestic, the choice is yours.

Intimate Freedom

*You are the director
of your play.*

*May love be your
inspiration, your cause,
and your recompense.*

*Truth for each person is
different because truth is
but the summary of the
individual's experiences.*

If you begin to feel manipulated, calmly remind yourself that:

1. You are free; totally free. The only ongoing restrictions are those that you've placed on yourself or agreed to.

2. Everyone has a right to live his own truth and individuality. So do you.

3. Whatever is lost along the way as you exercise freedom was never meant to be kept.

To concentrate deeply is to tap into the source of creativity. This is the place where original ideas are born. This is the location where truth, new ways of solving things, and understanding may be found.

With eyes closed, relax physically. Concentrate. Not outside of the body but bring the attention inside of the body. Keeping the eyes closed, concentrate and watch the "screen" between your eyes.

If the attention strays outside of the body, gently return your attention to the practice of watching within.

Try this technique during times of reflection alone or during lovemaking.

In war, man sends messages by bomb. The Great Mystery sends messages as gently as a butterfly.

Bombs are just an outward sign of humanity's collective inward strife. Reflect on the life cycle of a butterfly. Is that process what we are meant to do? When we, as individuals, will ourselves to break out from our own dark cocoon of ignorance; when we set ourselves free to exhibit our deeply unique beauty; when we tenaciously rise above the restrictions that we used to believe in, then, war will cease to exist.

However, it is the Great Journey of One; a journey from bondage to light.

Too much time is wasted reacting to what we believe others are thinking. Reacting to someone else's thoughts is to immediately forfeit one's power. It matters not how much you try to change, how you bend to adjust someone else's thoughts or appraisal of you, altering your behavior to appease someone else is always a mistake. By purposely modifying your conduct in order to try to please others, you lose yourself. Know that you will never have command over someone else's free will to think, feel or find fault with you, so since you can't control how someone else feels about you, why try?

Simply be the magnificent flower that you

are, remembering that flowers do not chase bees. The attracted bees will find you.

Dealing with the Pleasant and Unpleasant Within Us

I had a dream that began to recur. Each dream took place in a different setting, but the common theme was that I was being followed by what felt like a dark monster. I never turned around to see who or what was following me, but each night, that scary presence felt more ominous as I sought to escape it. Every time I had that dream, the creature would get closer and closer, leaving me more terrorized.

Finally, having had enough of it, I decided to take better control of my dream life. One night before going to sleep, instead of dreading that foreboding dream that might show itself, I vowed that when the frightening creature showed up, instead of escaping its' haunting presence, I would turn and face it. And so I did.

That night in the dream, I found myself in a grocery store pushing a shopping cart, when all of a sudden, I felt that awful presence close upon me. I turned wildly, and screamed, "What do you want?!" Instantly, the huge, dark monster turned into a tiny, sparkly pink fairy and hopped into the front of my shopping cart.

In my earthly, everyday life, I had been refraining from verbalizing certain negative things that had to be talked about to the people who were working for me. Never wanting to create hard feelings within the work environment, I held off communicating my dissatisfaction. Because I took the effort to understand the symbolism of my recent dream, it came to my realization that I did not wish to come across as a monster to my workers, even though the monster held unpleasant news that had to be conveyed and dealt with. I was running away from my responsibility to have the impending discussions and avoiding the talk, which caused the situation to become increasingly more troublesome in the workplace.

So, after the dream, I called a meeting where everyone in the workplace attended and my fear of being seen as a monster was overcome. I faced my co-workers and finally spoke about the subjects that were previously taboo and possibly hurtful, but the truth had to be told. After the meeting, instead of seeing myself as an ogre, I felt as light as a flying fairy. I've never had that dream again.

Acting on Your Truth

Jump from the diving board of compassion, then swim into each moment of your life.

If, before we take our next breath,
our next thought, our next step,
we are aware that we are coming
from a deep sense of kindness . . .
If we are honest and loving with ourselves,
if we are honest and loving toward others,
it then becomes impossible to take wrong
action.
Then, there is no such thing as a good act
or a bad act on our part.
There is only truth.
The truth of being who we really are.

Of course, that truth will change and evolve. But when it does, it will be timely and appropriate. Ultimately, this is the path to real freedom.

The Great Library

Before falling asleep, imagine that somewhere in your dream life there exists a Great Library. This library contains within it answers to all of your past, present, and future questions. Then carefully formulate a specific question and decide to visit the Great Library during your sleeping hours. Intend that you will not only awaken with a clear answer to your question but that you will also remember the information upon awakening. Finally, allow yourself to drift off to sleep. Begin an adventure into yourself.

Please don't give up if you aren't immediately successful. Try again and again before sleep. The strength of your determination will give you the results that you desire. It works.

P.S. Keep a pen, notepad and touch lamp by your bed. Write anything that comes to you as you awaken.

Things That Flow Into Our Lives

When feeling deep appreciation for all that you have in your life now, those genuine emotions of gratitude emit vibrations of an abundant nature. Those strong feelings go out and attract to themselves and into your life, that which is like itself. Consequently, experiences of richness and plenty will follow. The opposite is also true. If there is always a dwelling on deep strife, sorrow, scarcity and what seems to be missing in your life, those very emotions emit vibrations of a sad and vacant impoverished nature.

Those strong feelings go out and magnetize to themselves more of the same, and that is what will be experienced. Today's thoughts and emotions are creating tomorrow's experiences. What are you feeling right now? What are you setting yourself up to experience in the future?

The choice is yours.

When you ask for and plan on abundance, be prepared to release that which you have outgrown. Do not be surprised if suddenly unproductive relationships begin to fall away. There is no reason for alarm. You will sense that there must be a letting go or loosening of that which has hindered your higher options. These could be attachments to things or relationships. Room must be made in your life for new and more desirable circumstances. There should not be a blockage anywhere to deter the new from flowing in. You may taste the flavor of detachment before abundance, but all is in order.

One evening early in the 1980's, I found myself the victim of a very angry man. I had dated Frank for five and a half years. Never had I known him to exhibit extreme bouts of anger. On this particular evening, his birthday, I rushed out after work to meet him. He had been drinking, which was unusual enough even though he owned a partnership of a tavern. As soon as I arrived at his bar, he began to make venomous, accusatory remarks to me. Others became immediately uncomfortable. I was appalled and hurt at this unexpected and undeserved welcome. To my surprise, he asked his employees and customers to leave, although closing time was yet a half hour away.

I felt as if I was an ant scurrying for his ant hill or at least some grass to disappear in. My uneasiness grew as Frank glared at my every move. But how silly of me to worry. After all, this was someone I loved and trusted; someone who just had a little too much alcohol.

When the last person walked out, Frank locked the door, slipped the key into his pocket, and came after me. Grabbing my hair, he began to rhythmically bang my head against the brick wall of the tavern, all the while showing his teeth as a beast would do before attacking his prey. Half mad, he wrongly accused me of infidelity and feigning affection. This went on until finally I was left bewildered.

Almost a decade and a half after that incident, I had the following dream:

In another reincarnation, I see myself in Provence, France. I am with Frank. I cannot see his face, but I know it is him. He has me against the wall and is mad with rage but never sees his anger through. (End of dream.)

Perhaps finally, I might understand this uncharacteristic, bizarre behavior of my former companion.

Has someone "done us wrong?" Or are we the willing participants of cause and effect?

Upon reflection, have we been afraid that

some negative experience would befall us? If so, that particular fear has become a belief, and eventually we live out our beliefs.

More fundamentally, we may be harvesting the crop of unpleasantness that was seeded and cultivated in the past by none other than ourselves. As we probe deeper, let us ask, "Have there been times when we have caused others pain? Have we been unkind, apathetic, selfish and untruthful?" By and by, our thoughts and deeds come back to meet us.

Let us not omit the possibility that the offensive situations we find ourselves in could very well culminate in a significant and necessary life lesson.

Perhaps we have created the situation we find ourselves in and are, at this moment, creating blueprints for future circumstances. We have gotten what we've asked for through our beliefs, past actions or learning requirements.

It may be that we do ourselves wrong.

Expend the Least Amount of Energy (or Money) to Achieve the Greatest Result

Those possessing a great deal of wealth but are cautious or frugal enough to appreciate a bargain aren't necessarily stingy (although there are exceptions). They have a strong belief in wealth and in their ability to always be abundant, yet they moderate their spending at times because of the pleasure that comes from the anticipation of spending, and from the feeling of knowing what money can do. Those feelings of security, knowing that money is there and available, draw even more wealth for them to experience in the future. Therefore, they may be conservative with it in mundane areas so that they may be free to delegate generously of their wealth where it guarantees the most joy.

Those who have little and can barely survive yet give everything away are not always generous. It is impossible for them to possess riches or hang on to them for long because they don't believe that they are abundant.

Money Was Always Difficult to Come By in Early Years

I used to believe that to be poor was to be godly. Being the head of household, I felt that because money was scarce, my family depended on me a great deal for survival. At the time, I rather liked that. This was the way it should be. After all, my forefathers lived this way. I would feel guilty if I had more than they did. They suffered, why shouldn't I?

One way or another, I found ways to financially sabotage myself. I couldn't have too much money because everyone would lose their perspectives. If there was more money to go around, my family wouldn't need me as much. To make matters worse, I thought I would no longer be as holy because I'd be so comfortable that I'd have no reason to stop and pray for help.

I was wrong. My life has completely turned for the better because I changed my mind, my beliefs and my expectations.

When you examine and correct the direction

of the beliefs and expectations that you hold, your life will improve also. You have nothing to lose and everything to gain.

Don't Give to the Undeserving or Unappreciative

Giving is an art. So is receiving also an art. Throughout our lives, we find ourselves refining both.

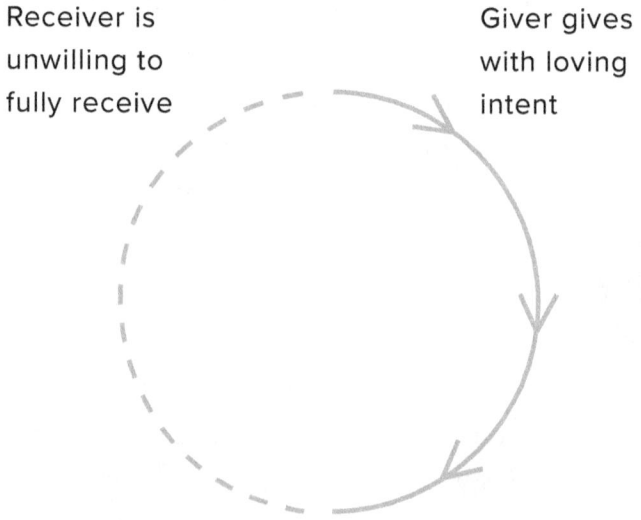

Receiver is unwilling to fully receive

Giver gives with loving intent

The energy circle of giving is dissipated.

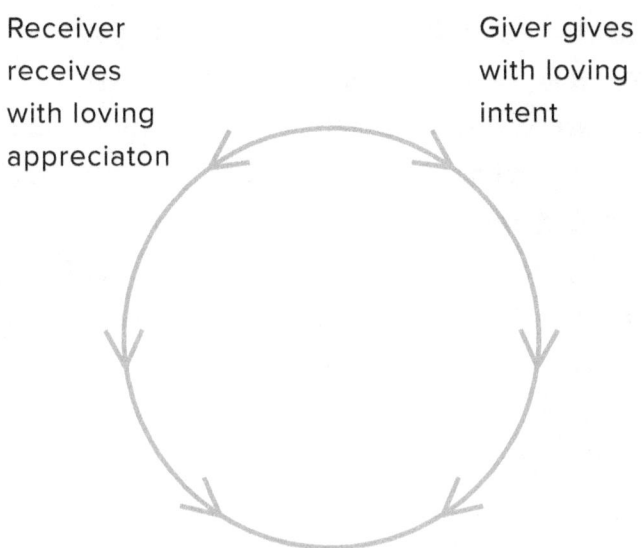

Receiver receives with loving appreciaton

Giver gives with loving intent

The energy circle of giving is complete.

As illustrated on the previous page, one can see how vitally important the act of receiving is in the context of completing the energy circle. As seen in the top circle the direction and movement of the arrows demonstrate that the receiver is unwilling to fully receive, thus the energy circle of giving and receiving is dissipated. The bottom diagram represents the energy circle being completed. You can also see how vitally important the act of receiving is in the context of completing the energy circle.

Always give freely, without thought of recompense. It is not necessary to know whom you are giving to personally, only know that you are open as a vacuum. Give of kindness, patience, money, forgiveness, energy, material goods, time, prayer, and understanding. Give where and when you are moved to share. Give unabashedly and outrageously.

But be wise in your giving. Remember to provide for others only as much generosity as can readily be taken in and utilized by them. If the receivers think themselves unworthy or if they are uninterested in your gift, the circle is broken. Do not give where the fullness of your gift is not amply appreciated, or you may feel frustration because the activity of the circle is temporarily incomplete.

While it is true that unrequited caring (or giving) will eventually flow back to the giver, it usually takes more time. Your responsibility in the role of the receiver is this: It is not necessary to know who has given to you. Words or actions on your part are not always needed. All that is required is honest appreciation. Accept graciously. Welcome what flows to you as a deserving child of the Universe. Spare not your feelings of inner gratitude. Bring forth and focus on the abundance and wellness of your being. Know that you are an integral part of a great kingdom. Fill yourself with these heartfelt feelings, for they are now your gift to present. They will flow back to the original giver who will become the recipient. The circle will then be complete.

In the final analysis, giving freely and receiving freely are but two aspects of the same phenomenon. They are one. Such is the circle of life.

Everything Is Always Working Out for the Best for Me— Believe and Repeat It

When you are feeling scared, it becomes more difficult to hear guidance. Any ominous and fearfully fueled thought of tomorrow is the slamming door that blocks divine assistance. When you are feeling surprised or frightened, stop for a moment and although you cannot see the whole picture from above, KNOW that everything is always working out for the best for you. Practice saying, **"Everything is always working out for the best for me."** Continue repeating that until you feel the certainty and sureness of it. Then, maintain trusting hopefulness. It is the magnet that draws intuitive support and direction.

———————— ✦ ————————

It was a bright summer day and a friend and I sat in the yard. Mike, an elderly neighbor, made his way over and gifted us with a fresh bunch of large pink flowers from his yard. He was proud of those flowers.

Watching him walk away, one couldn't help but feel touched at the simplicity and purity of the moment. My friend rose to complete a task that had previously started that day, leaving me alone with the smiling pink blossoms. I asked the flowers, "Teach me something. What can you teach me?"

I felt their answer.

The very act of pruning a plant, cutting the flowers away to be enjoyed, causes the plant to bring forth even more blossoms in place of the ones cut off. So must we use the blossoms and fruits of our own labor, giving them away and enjoying them. In this fashion shall we continue to allow abundance to flow in our lives.

Whatever you want in your own life, give freely.

Gratitude begets abundance.
Calmness begets peace.
Non-expectation begets non-judgment.
Love begets affection.
Thoughtfulness begets clarity.
Well-being begets joy.
Aestheticism begets order.
Dwell on these things.

Changing
Directions

When It Is Time to
Change Direction

You are the director of your play. May love be your inspiration, your cause, and your reward.

Think of the conscience functioning in the same manner as a metal detector. When the detector that is our conscience "beeps" with guilt, it is a message that says, "Going the wrong way.

This action is not in the best interests of Life." Mentally thank the conscience for the discomfort of its warning and turn away to go in another direction.

Turn away, also, from any feelings of guilt. We abuse our conscience by refusing to forgive ourselves for taking a wrong turn. Denying ourselves forgiveness then becomes a transgression against our nature and our well-being.

We were never meant to carry the debilitating burden of our guilt forever. We are to experience guilt only as long as it takes us to realize that we're not acting on behalf of the highest ideal within us. Once this is realized, conscience has done its' job. We can then let go of our past wrongdoings. Drop the guilt with a knowing that we will find a more comfortable path as we turn to walk a new direction. Keep on walking until the conscience detector beeps again. It's really as simple as that.

Think on This

The body reacts the same way to fear
as it does to excitement.
The next time you're feeling afraid,
try thinking, "I'm excited."
When the fear is gone,
the excitement is gone.

Some people need fear.
Tormented because
your mind is racing?

Slow down the mind
by slowing the breath.

I repeat—Slow down the mind
by slowing the breath.

Inhale deeply through the nose then exhale a little slower through the mouth. Continue doing this until you are feeling calm and centered. Once you are settled down, take your next step from this place of clarity.

Stability can be seen as an exception rather than the rule. Is stability a fallacy? Have you noticed that nothing remains the same, and that everything is always in a state of flux and changing non-stop? This is the way of Earth life, yet much of the emotional pain that we experience comes because we get upset that something that we wished to remain the same, has become different in some way.

Since we cannot ever stop change, why fight it? Let us try instead, to become malleable and allow ourselves to have softer edges. Adaptation is an important key to living an easier existence.

Don't Look Back

Live out of your imagination instead of your memory. Pay Attention to Your Unique Personal Signs from the Universe.

My husband loved numbers. One of his major studies was statistics and logic. I, on the other hand, would rather focus on aestheticism and beauty in the world. Opposites attract.

I noticed during the day that in random places, I was seeing sets of at least three of the same number. When this began, these numbers were catching my attention about three or four times a day. I enjoyed the coincidences. As the weeks went by, the frequency of times that I was seeing these sets of numbers was increasing. A month later, I was aware of these different sets of numbers showing themselves to me at least ten times a day. Two months had passed since the first time I noticed these phenomena got my attention, but the frequency of seeing them continued to increase. I was now seeing these numbers 20 to 22 times a day.

The charm I once felt over this phenomenon began to feel eerie. When I asked my husband's opinion of what he thought these appearances in our world meant, he said that he was not aware and had noticed nothing of the sort. He reminded me that he was the one who was the "numbers guy" and asked, "Since when have you been interested in numbers?" I answered, "I am not interested in them at all. They are interested in me!" He did not understand, so

I said that instead of keeping my observations to myself, I would point them out to him when we were together.

Since he was home from a business trip, we happily set out for a day of enjoyment. He filled the car's tank with gas, and we drove toward the movie theater. At our first traffic stop I pointed to a house on the corner and asked, "What is the house number on that building?" He said, "444." At the next stop, I asked him to please read the mile marker number on the side of the road. He read, "222," and then smiled at me.

We parked under a tree at the end of a row of cars in the theater, then rushed in to see a movie. When the movie was over, we decided to sit through the music and read some of the film's end credits. Almost everyone walked out during that time except for one man and us. Suddenly, the screen showed a solid black background with the numbers 666 in big bold white contrast. My husband and I looked at each other and he half-jokingly said that this was weird.

When we sat ourselves back into the car and started the engine, we noticed that the gas gauge was very close to the empty mark and deduced that since we had parked in a semi-private area, someone had siphoned our gas while we were gone. Luckily, there was a gas station close by, and he filled the tank for the second time that day while I went to a restaurant to get a bite to eat. The bill came to $77.77.

Later that evening, my husband and I were watching a DVD. He had to take a break and paused the DVD. This time it was he who noticed and then said to me, "Take a look at where it paused." The numbers showed 1:11.

Many times, I would look at a clock and see 5:55, 4:44, 3:33, 2:22 or 1:11, sometimes being awakened only for a moment to draw my attention to the clock by my bed. (These numerical coincidences continued relentlessly over the next few weeks.)

The next day, we set out again to see another film at a different movie house than the day before on another side of town. This time, my husband chose to park in a very visible area, unlike the spot we parked in the day before. Upon leaving the theater, we found that our car's gas gauge was again showing that the tank was empty.

In the morning, my husband left for an up-coming business trip to several different locations. Meanwhile, the sight of the sequences of numbers was growing more and more frequent, leaving me wondering. A few days before the culmination of his journey, we spoke on the phone. He told me that when he returns from this trip, he wants to quit his job and that it was his wish for the two of us that we begin a new life. It was a meaningful conversation about selling our home, downsizing, and starting over. We pledged our commitment to each other to move in new directions and ended the phone call.

About fourteen seconds later, as I was walking away, something impelled me to turn around and call him back. When he answered, I said, "I just want to reiterate that I will always love you. I want you to know that no matter what, I will forever hold you up and will never let you down. I will always be not only by your side, but behind you. I want you to be sure of these things." He answered, "I'm glad because I need to know that before I do what I'm about to do."

Twenty minutes later, my husband died suddenly of a stroke. He had told me several times before his death that he wished to be buried next to his father, whose grave was across the country from where we lived. Ironically, that is where my husband gave up his life, very close to his father's grave site.

At the funeral wake a friend of mine, whose husband had also died, approached me and said, "Did you see the 1111? After my husband died, I saw 1111 everywhere! It means that everything is as it should be." She left me speechless.

A few weeks later, my brother sent me the cards from the people who had sent flowers to the funeral home. Most of the flowers came from the same florist whose business was very close by. All of the cards from that particular florist had the same embossed, not stamped with ink, florist's information containing the name, address and phone number of the business. Every card was alike except the last one I looked at. That last card also had the same embossed information of the florist, with the florist's business name, but the address imprint of the building was listed as 1111 instead of the actual address number. Also, the telephone number was not the correct number listed on all of the other cards. The telephone number listed on this card was 111-111-1111.

As when transcribing a dream, I looked back at the symbolism of those two days in a row, when my husband filled the gas tank, only to find that the tank was empty shortly thereafter. Was life telling us that my husband was "running out of gas" too soon?

What about the numbers? They finally slowed down after my husband died, but over time, I have come to realize that for me personally, when the number sequences start to ramp up and again begin to show themselves to me very frequently, I now translate the messages to mean, "Brace yourself. Something is coming that will affect your life. There is a bigger plan that you cannot see. Brace yourself and know that you are not alone."

In contrast, I have noticed in my experience, that when seeing these sequences of numbers infrequently during a day, it seems to indicate an affirmative nod for what I am doing or where I am going or who I am with, reminding me that I am never alone.

Pay attention to the signs that the Universe gives you to decipher. As in dreams, each symbol represents a personal meaning to the dreamer. The interpretation of life's signs will be yours and unlike anyone else's. Relax. How about making as few plans and as few choices as possible. Then, let Life show you what it wants to be.

To fight anything is to give it life. But to embrace it will result in its' transformation. Look at it without emotion. Permanently turn your attention away. Only then does one overcome the conflict.

Instead of praying or begging for something visualize in your mind a complete picture of what you want. Then flood that picture with loving light and let Creation work its magic.

The struggle has died. You are free.

Embracing the Word, "YES" Will Lead You to Places and Things that You Didn't Realize You Wanted

Holistic growth is a balance between spiritual betterment and acknowledging the divinity of our naturalness. It is the appreciation of those urgings and whims that we possess. While meditation and similar tools can be comforting, they are not enough if used only to appease oneself in consistently distressful situations. If we long for a more supportive life, change is the answer.

One way to begin to improve our life situations through change is by bringing to our awareness those parts of ourselves that we brush off, don't take seriously or sometimes ignore. It is done by taking the time to sense, to hear, to know our deep desires that periodically emerge and are the guideposts toward a blossomed character. Once we are clear about our goals, we can then take steps to bring them to fruition. Those who persevere in this area, exercise their godliness.

The combination of self-rediscovery and impartial respect toward all aspects of our naturalness of mind, body, and spirit are catalysts for serious development.

Sometimes, we must stop doing what we think we should do, and instead, do what is more natural and comforting in the moment. Honor yourself. Say "yes" to your inclinations more often. You won't get lost.

The "past" could be one hundred years ago. One minute ago, is as valid a part of the past as one hundred years ago.

The past has passed.

That being so, can we truly let the past go and begin once more anew?

If you would like to understand someone more completely or wish to know better how someone feels, try this simple practice:

- Study whomever you are interested in.

- Mentally place yourself into that person's body.

- Try to look out of their eyes.

- Attempt to feel what it is that they are hoping for.

You will discover that it is quite easy to experience another's reality. When done sincerely, this experiment will result in a more forgiving, more tolerant, more compassionate you.

If your choice is to study a personality whose qualities you aspire to, mentally merge with that individual often. Eventually you will learn to be like them.

Happiness as Medicine

What to do next? Think about what originally interested you as a child as hints pointing to what you may be meant to work on in this lifetime before the world told you that you could not. Be mindful of the activities that strongly beckon. Which of them cause time to pass most quickly? Ask, "What feels like the most comfortable of all possible choices in this moment?" Know that by the contentment, peace and voluntary attention that you freely give to an activity, your direction shall be shown.

Notice that some of society is beginning to reward the populace who does not succumb to disease and depression. People who are happy most of the time find themselves having few visits to doctors or psychologists. The more joy one will allow oneself to live with, the less need to see doctors. Let us study the relationship between happiness and health.

If significant amounts of humanity's education involved the study of how to maintain contentment and cheer in one's life, the world could evolve much quicker because humans would have the time and energy to enjoy forward movement in their lives instead of being bogged down with health ailments.

There was a period when, to maintain a license, I had to go through a yearly physical with a medical doctor. He asked me what my secret was to keeping low blood pressure and good health. At the time, I had been engaged in daily meditation and told him I felt that was the reason. He haughtily dismissed the mere idea that such a way could be possible, but for some, this can be true.

Who will begin to design and implement a healthcare plan that works like this: Should someone become ill and need medical care, the sick person will pay in order to cure his illness, however, if a taxpayer goes one year with no medical bills, the government pays him as a reward for staying healthy.

What fulfills you? Do it! Live it! Enjoy each precious moment of allowing those things into your daily life. Joy is contagious and such powerful medicine.

If whatever is annoying or bothering you begins to take up more energy than you're comfortable donating, try thinking about the larger scheme of things and ask these two questions:

1. Twenty-five years from now, how much will this matter?

2. During the final hour of my life, how significant will this be?

Don't wait for time. Drop the baggage off now.

Instructions for Living

Imagine night lights as being symbols for a portion of our earthly opportunity. You know those little plug-in lights that, in essence, perform a big job. After all, they function to show the way. They dispel confusion and fear. They save time and perhaps the pain of a fall. They bring feelings of well-being. They guide and illumine.

We humans are filled with light and yet how

often do we dare to fully expose the sun of our nature upon others?

Shed a little light in the darkness of someone's life. Do it often. Grace us. Become a night light unto our world.

Relationships Should Be Run Like an Investment Portfolio

Never invest your entire life's energy in any one place or in any one person. It's too risky. Forgiveness.

To achieve the state of forgiveness seems to be an insurmountable task. Do you sometimes feel as if you have tried to forgive someone, but deep down inside, knowing the truth, you are aware that forgiveness in fact, has not happened at all?

If forgiveness is an impossible feat, here is the way to conquer unforgiveness: Never look back at what offended you. Do not give it any more power in your life. Just don't look back.

Then, without effort, forgiveness is already behind you, but without a name. Done.

Your Feet Upon the Earth Is Enough

Our relationship to God is not a weekly wor-
ship service or a daily time of prayer and meditation, but a minute-by-minute walk with that
Great Encompassor who is always present. It
is always present, and we are not apart from It.
It is a spark that exists within us. You adjust
yourself as you would to hear a particular ra-
dio station. Make sure that you're always tuned
in and listening with intention. Leading from
this place your footsteps will be divinely led.
You don't need to argue with anyone anymore.
The best form of persuasion is by leading with
a good example.

Rise to the knowledge and the responsibility
of being a representative of the body of God.
Face all things with the power of thunder radiating from your heart and through your eyes.
Know yourself to be the Lighthouse in the

storm. It is now time to come into fullness as a member of the Universe, having come to this planet to be a tuning fork of peace as you walk upon the Earth. You are the energy beam of refuge, a searchlight of God showing the way. By your existence, by your presence alone, do you hold the torch for all who seek. Wherever you go, is forever transformed. You know how to be who you are. Nothing else is needed.

Fear can paralyze us or we can use fear as a temporary tool to positively influence our lives. Here is an example:

- **Identify the fear: "What am I afraid of?"** *Sometimes I have a hard time hearing. I fear that I may go deaf.*

- **Feel the fear in all its intensity: "Allow myself to enter and consciously move through it."** *I acknowledge the fear. I feel it.*

- **Ask, "If this fear were to manifest, how would my life change?"** *If I were deaf, I would no longer have to listen to* *the nagging, complaining, and distaste-ful conversations in my life; however, I wouldn't hear the lovely ones either. I would definitely have needed much quiet time, but there would be too much.*

Conclusion: I don't need to be deaf. If I can learn to move away from people and circumstances that I don't want to listen to, and if I will make more time for peacefulness and quiet in my life, I won't need to manifest deafness. By moving through our fears, we take our fear to its limit, and then, the glorious part: We Walk out the other end. We move past the worry and fear of "what if" and take it through to, "I don't need to be deaf" (or whatever it is that we're afraid of). We can utilize the positive aspects of what we've learned and replace our paralyzing fears with a clear plan for an improved future.

Our spines are like flowing springs.
We spout energy up through them
as a lively water fountain does.

Taking the highest action in any
given moment could be as simple
as just straightening one's posture.

How to Leap Forward and Live More Comfortably Without Wasting the Energy of Indecision

One of my young dinner companions came home feeling very ill. I said to him, "I am going to ask you a question, then I want you to quickly and without thinking or reasoning, blurt out the first thought that comes into your mind." I said, "What is making you sick right now?" He blurted out, "That FISH that I ate!" I snapped my fingers and said, "There! That is your intuition at work, and it is always correct and true."

When a thought flashes into your mind, pay attention! It is that first glimmering of an idea that is your divine guidance. Don't dismiss your first notion, or decide, "No, that was just my imagination." Before the thought is tackled down with doubt and confusion, honor what came into your awareness. Don't begin to over-think the thought that you had. Do not judge what was shown to you. Don't go on a tangent wondering and fancying other options. The time wasted in going through the "Should I, or shouldn't I? This way or that way?" will no longer happen. You will walk with a sureness of step and have faith in your decisions because they come from a higher perspective of you.

Your guidance system is always working. Trust it and the way to trust it is to act on that first quick hint that came to you. As you live in this manner, acting as you are shown, you will hear and feel more clearly, and your guidance will seem to get stronger (although it is always there, but ignored or not given precedence).

When in doubt, go back and remember the very first thought that came to you. That's the way to go.

Be a gracious listener with others.

Be a gracious listener when alone.

*It is ill-mannered to ceaselessly force
one's own thoughts upon the ethers.
Instead make the effort to get quiet.
Then listen deeply.*

---

*Try to keep laughing more
—especially at yourself.*

How does it benefit me to have ideals but not apply them?

Let me view life as a gift; an opportunity to apply what I've learned. I cannot move forward until I've proven myself as worthy. Now is my opportunity. Each moment is a new beginning.

Protection

A wildly, angry, bullish man started toward me fast, with violence in his eyes. Strangely, I watched him, arms up, stopped as if by a wall of invisible glass. He backed up stunned, and meekly stepped away, leaving me out of reach of his intended harm.

On another occasion, a friend confided that he was not comfortable inside of his home where he and his girlfriend lived. Also, he felt uneasy in his workplace office. We talked about the possibility that his home and work area might need some spiritual refreshment. He asked if I would join him in opening to move energy through him. He planned on holding fresh energy and radiating it throughout his home. When he arrived at the house, he walked around with intentions of spiritually cleansing the area. As he did, he began to feel ill and lay on the couch. His discomfort grew and he rolled off of the couch onto the floor writhing in discomfort. When his girlfriend arrived home, he called out to her for help. She quickly went to him, only to be stopped by what seemed to be an invisible wall of glass.

He told her to call a trusted friend who immediately came over to the house to pray. Soon afterwards, he felt better, the invisible barrier was gone and the home felt light and airy once again. After some contemplation, he realized it was his girlfriend who needed spiritual cleansing. He took her to Mexico, where an exorcism was performed.

We're never alone. Always trust that the divine protects us when It is called upon.

I awaken to morning music in my head. Contentment and fullness are mine as I stir. Where have I journeyed last night as my body slept? Is this a glimpse of heaven that I'm feeling? The peace of the universe? I will try to preserve this state and carry it into the day as long as possible, for my joy drains as I allow worldly thoughts to flood my consciousness.

*True and lasting beauty would never
compete, for it is born within.*

*Perhaps that is why "inner beauty
pageants" are non-existent.*

When you decide to interact with someone, watch what happens when you look that person straight in the eye without wavering your gaze. Listening with full attention, hold your posture well and perhaps lean in an inch toward that person. If there is true honesty, that person will begin to blossom before your very eyes.

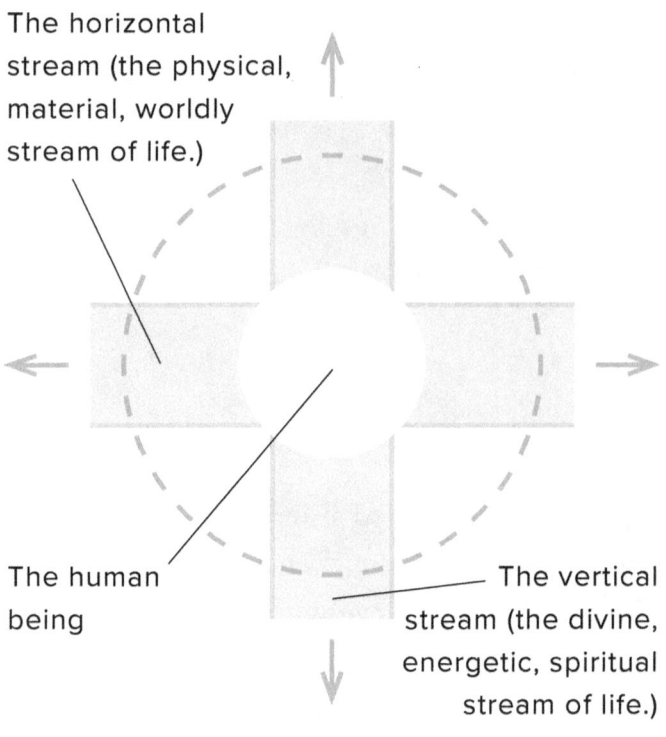

The horizontal stream (the physical, material, worldly stream of life.)

The human being

The vertical stream (the divine, energetic, spiritual stream of life.)

The vertical bars in the diagram of the cross represent the ever flowing, ever changing Divine stream of life. The horizontal bars represent the ever flowing, ever transmuting earthly or physical stream of life. Metaphorically, we are the circle at the intersection of the cross. We exist in both worlds, where both streams meet. We experience transitory divine life and transitory physical life simultaneously.

Because of the constant, yet dissimilar

motion of both streams, it is impossible to resist change. No two moments can ever be the same. It is our challenge as human beings to remain centered as all life moves through us and by us. We are called to focus on the present moment and to resist traveling too far on either stream of life.

This is how to live your life.

Each day be the hands of your Creator.

When encountering an acquaintance, think not of his faults, but of his most notable deed. Then treat that person according to his highest point of action. This encourages the receiver and softens the giver.

Mastering the art of presenting a sincere compliment is a worthy achievement. Such behavior renders hope in the receiver and is also becoming to the giver. Others wish to be viewed affirmatively through the giver's eyes, which always cheers the evolution of goodness.

Let us decide that a greater percentage of everything we say shall be complimentary. Shall we begin today?

———— ✦ ————

Live each day with a song
on your lips, encouragement in your
voice, love in your eyes, and joy in
your heart.

———— ✦ ————

I recall Buddha, who led himself to enlightenment. Are we, each of us, on respective journeys leading ourselves toward enlightenment? We are sometimes compelled to follow our own consciences toward what we feel that we could trust in.

Perhaps there are signs or symbols that cause us to immediately feel that we are never without contact with a deep and benevolent side of our consciousness. What names or traditions bring you a feeling of protection?

Hearing the name, Christ, I think of the man, Jesus, who became the Christ, or Christos, the Anointed One.

One evening, I awoke in my bed feeling afraid and uncomfortable. Quickly, I sat up and tried looking around. Even though the night light was plugged in and the hallway light should have been showing under my door, I realized that I was in complete darkness. There was no illumination anywhere. My eyes were open, but I could see only absolute darkness. Wanting to understand what was happening, I found that I could not move my body from the waistline, down to my feet. The bottom of my body was paralyzed. I began to feel helpless against this sinister feeling that seemed to be encroaching upon me.

I remembered being told that the crucifix, a symbol for Jesus Christ, could be a protective talisman. Since I could still move my upper body, I used the forefingers of my right and left hands to form a symbol of a crucifix, one vertical finger and another horizontal finger on top. I began to say, "Jesus, Jesus, Jesus, Jesus . . ." as I held my hands in the position of the cross. Soon, it was as if a black shade that had been hanging down from ceiling to floor, began to lift. Slowly lifting the dark from the floor, up, I could begin to see glimmers of light coming into the room. The light was beginning to be seen again, but I still could not move the lower half of my body. The black shade of darkness continued to slowly lift as I continued to repeat the name of Jesus and still holding my fingers crossed. As the dark curtain proceeded to lift, the sight of the lit room began to rise. When the visible light rose up high enough to reach the top of my bed where I sat, and the black shade went higher, the light reached my legs. Once the lower part of my body was no longer in darkness, I was able to move again.

Unpleasant as it may be, there is never enough reason to be bound by negative energy. You are your own version of the God or belief system that is of your choosing. Never forget your power.

Search for godliness in everyone

*When encountering an acquaintance,
think not of his faults, but of his
most notable deed.
Then treat that person according to
his highest point of action.
This encourages the receiver
and softens the giver.*

Then, search for godliness everywhere else.

Solidarity

No man is an island unto himself. Imagine each of us as a tiny cell in the giant body of humanity. Each of us as cells performs our own unique function in our own way; hence, the body of the giant is healthy and strong. Of course, there is no prejudice or malice between the cells of the foot and the cells of the shoulder. The body has an innate desire toward solidarity. Should some of us fall into a period of prolonged self-ishness, guilt, unforgiveness, anger, hatred, lethargy, or any emotion that results in our being ill at ease, we would eventually manifest as disease-filled cells.

Functioning naturally, the rest of the body would come to the rescue of the few diseased cells, striving to heal and cleanse itself. The last thing the giant body of humanity wants is for anything to impede its' progress.

We, in our turn, must do the same to our ailing, wrongdoing brother and sister cells. Without competition, let us make haste to assist, to understand, to make peace with, and thus heal them so that we may be healed and free.

There is only us, our, we.

---

*The manner in which one treats
others is equivalent to the way
one feels about the Divine or Oneself.*

The Divine
Seeks Fulfillment Also

Each man holds within himself a flame, which is a portion of God.

We are important and influential to the Almighty Being.

When our lives are meaningful there is fulfillment for God.

The tangerine tree was not doing very well in the backyard. It was slow growing and bore no fruit. When my father, Mario, came to town from the cold climate that he lived in, the tree caught his attention. He asked, "What is wrong with that tree?" "I don't know," I replied. My father spent a lot of time sitting in the backyard, looking at that tree. After about three days, he said, "I know what that tree wants."

My father dug a twelve-inch-deep ditch in the dirt around the perimeter of the tree. The ditch was located directly below where the farthest reach of the tree's leaves hung in the air. He loosened all of the soil. Then he got down on his hands and knees, and with his big rough hands, he began to mix the soil around the tree.

He continued, moving around the tree several times, stirring the soil silently. About forty-five minutes later, my father stood up, and with a shovel, packed the dirt back around the tree.

Let me convey to you, reader, that tree began to grow with vital power. The following seasons, the tree was fecund with superior, highly, sweet tasting tangerines producing a great abundance of fruit. Each year while in his frigid weather, he would receive a big box of those sunny, delicious tangerines in the mail, enjoying the fruit of his empathy with that tree.

A familial relatedness will be felt toward any concept or object that is given individual and prolonged concentration. Try it now and understand.

We Are All Connected;
We Are One

As long as we focus our attention on or from the tiniest point of our being—our waking consciousness, we seem very separate do we not?

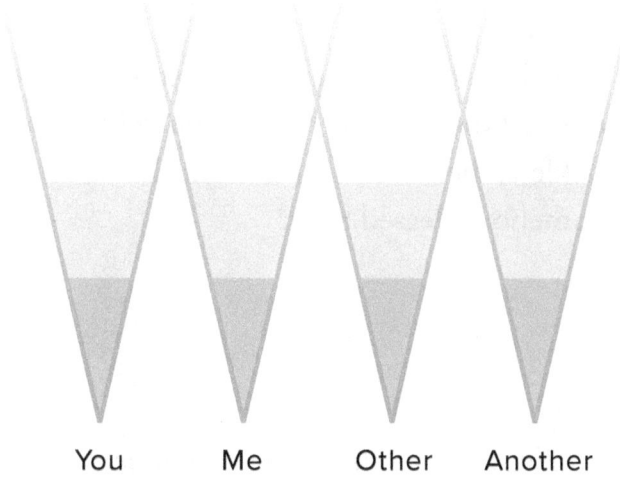

You   Me   Other   Another

Waking Consciousness (the personality that we show to the everday world)

The Subconscious Mind

The Superconsciousness (where we are indivisily one)

The subconscious areas of our being still seem very separate from the next person.

Studying the figure above, we can see that as we "loosen the grip" of our personalities, perhaps through deep meditation, sleep or the natural dream state, we expand into our Higher Selves where there exists no separation, no delineation. The greater parts of ourselves

merge and melt into one ocean of unified consciousness.

In reality, can we cause pain to another without somehow causing pain to ourselves? Is it
possible to bestow love unto another and not
be somehow blessed by it?

Even in war, there are no winners.

*It is impossible to intentionally
harm others without doing some
measure of harm to ourselves.*

I am you.
You are me.
Therefore, we are one.

The Mind is the Builder

All attainments of civilization originated in the minds of humans. We imagine a work of art, an architectural structure, a meal, a hair style, a garden, a society. Then we manifest our dreams. We create. We build. What was once a thought takes form.

Who imagined us? Was humankind once only a thought in a mind? Who dreamed us?

You will not be able to solve your problems as long as you are in the same mindset as you were in when the problem was created.

Change your mind to fix the problem.

Making the Most of Our Time

Bang! A fast thought shines through your being. You have just experienced multidimensionality.

Immediately, the mind begins to argue against that first blush of the idea that just crossed your mind. You have just experienced the conscious level of your being.

After that, one begins to question or mentally argue against the mind's limited capabilities, thinking things such as, "No, I can't do it that way. Maybe it should be done this way. Or, that has never been done like this before, so it can't work now."

Then, you move from your initial flash of knowing into doubt and uncertainty, where progress slows and time, precious time is wasted. When you find yourself going off on a tangent in several directions because you are not sure of which way to turn, think back to your very first initial thought about the subject you are wondering about. That first impression is giving you the most accurate information to base your decision on. That is the correct way to go.

Here is a revolutionary, evolutionary way to begin living right now when listening for guidance:

Forget everything you've ever known.

In other words, see everything with new expectation, yes, new possibility, a new way, take an unknown road. Stop second guessing your initial thoughts that pop up immediately before the mind begins to challenge them. Those initial quick impressions are always showing you the truth.

When a flash of knowledge quickly drops into your awareness, trust it. **That is your intuition.**

When wishing for an event or manifestation, it is not enough to simply form a mental image of the outcome. You must be able to smell it, taste it, hear it, and feel the emotions that will accompany what you are hoping for. The "picture" should be detailed and the senses aroused.

Then, like the blinding light of a flashcube, mentally flood the scene with illumination. That being done, go about your day and repeat as necessary.

Let us direct our minds toward the highest, most expansive thoughts we can imagine during free moments. Let us fill ourselves.

I seek to acknowledge the essence in you that is also in me. We are made of the same divine fire. If we are going to become what we think about, if what we give out will return back to us, why not give acceptance, an approving nod, a loving gaze? Find and look at the magic that lives in the individuals around us, and in all facets of nature. Seek a divine quality in all things and in everyone. Let us remember that we become what we think about.

Look at the disappointing side of things only for a moment, but don't dwell on them. Instead, notice at least one thing that is of good report, any complimentary aspect of someone around you. That is what will begin to expand.

When someone notices that we are looking at them, how we feel toward them radiates from our faces and reflects back to the person we are looking at. Many people look for their approval or disapproval of themselves based on how our faces appear when we look at them.

When coming across people, gaze upon them with warm loving eyes. Send them a feeling of the love that is your essence. If a person is aware, he or she will immediately feel your approval, and continue on their day, uplifted. Let us reflect joyful acceptance to those who briefly gaze upon us in passing. Make their day light and easy simply by wearing an expression of approval on your face as you pass them. By your demeanor, are you the mirror showing others their worthiness.

Think of each thought you have as a boomerang always returning back to you, affecting you with the original intentions that you sent it out with. Knowing that your original thoughts and intentions are returning to you, how do they feel?

Turn Your Thoughts Inside

As though your thoughts were being worn outside of you, think like that.

As if each thought was publicly heard, think like that.

Concepts employed by the mind, manifest.

You are growing toward that which you consider.

Aspire to occupy the mind with ideas of honor, fairness, trustworthiness.

Why not be undefiled?

Whatever God means to you, pretend for a time that you are God.

As God, how do you think?

How do you see?

How do you touch?

How do you feel?

How do you act?

Knowing the answers to these questions and putting that knowledge into practice will transform not only your life but everything around you.

Stand On Your Own Two Feet Today

What more courageous an act is there than that of a person who can step back to look at oneself, one's creations, one's fears, and one's beliefs, and say,

"I am responsible."

Some poignant advice was once given to me by my brother, Sal, during a very low period of my life. How wise he is. He said, "You are your own best friend. You have yourself." The fullness of Sal's statement was hidden when I was younger. Time has enabled me to understand. This is what his counsel, given so long ago, means to me today.

> *"You are your own best friend.*
> *You have yourself."*

There is nowhere else to run but here. There is ultimately no one else to turn to but me. All the answers lie within. Although I may wish to share with others now and then, the only companionship I am truly in need of is my whole, aware, deep self. For at the end, that is who will be with me.

At this point of my evolution, searching for a spiritual leader to guide me would only bring repetitive frustration. Disappointment will always ensue if I continue to look outside myself for fulfillment or answers to my most pressing questions. I am happy to announce, "It is all here. All needs can be met if I would but patiently excavate deeper into myself; if I would but diligently listen further inward. If I am all there is to turn to, then the idea that I could not live holistically without various others or things was an illusion."

Realizing this brings new responsibility. Afterwards, life cannot be the same. When you know that you're complete within yourself, you can never again be with another out of neediness if you're honest. Nor will you feel compelled to strive for anything. The essence of it is already here.

Once we choose to exercise our natural ability to think and live in the lofty spaces of our conscience, we become less affected by the mundane world at large. Even temptations gradually lose their glitter.

Have you felt let down by the people you love? Are you disappointed that those dear to you may not have responded the way you hoped they would?

There could be a lesson here. Think deeply. Is it possible that for every disloyalty shown to you by others, prior to that disappointment, you may have been disloyal to yourself? Each time someone thought you weren't important enough, able enough, special enough, is it because you've had those very same thoughts about yourself? When backs were turned and you were forgotten, think back. Had you ever turned away from fully acknowledging your own abilities.

What else could possibly manifest but indifference and rejection if you have convicted your own self? The time has come to give yourself permission to be wonderful. Give yourself permission now. You are the only one who can. Rise to self-honor, self-trust, self-love, self-referral, and allegiance to your heart's callings.

Others do not place you before themselves, as it should be. Learn to put yourself first.

From this moment onward, dedicate your

life to You. Know yourself to be a powerful entity able to create many, many possibilities. You
are free. Unbound.

Now move on.

Success at helping others
through their hardships comes
only after we've learned to be
with our own.

If not here, then where?
If not at this point in time, when?
If not me, who?

It has been observed in monkeys that when a
new way of doing something is learned by one
monkey in one place on Earth, the other monkeys of that same tribe watch and learn the

same new habit. Through example, more and more in the tribe begin to employ the new trait that the first monkey exhibited.

Once the number of monkeys who are taught the new way of doing something reaches the critical number of 100, a turning point within the evolution of that species occurs across the entire planet. For the first time, that species of monkey is then born, although thousands of miles away, with the instinctive new intelligence of the trait started on the other side of the planet. With just 100 monkeys having learned the same new trait that was unknown to them in the past, the newly birthed monkeys possess the instinctual abilities to perform the new traits naturally that began across the globe, without having been taught or shown.

It seems that once a critical mass of knowing is accumulated, it becomes available to all. As humanity refines itself to more peaceful ways of existing, we can transform life as we now know it. When we prove ourselves to be ready for new inventions that will be utilized only for the betterment of the planet, not for the detriment of the Earth, and life upon it, the

Universe will respond favorably. These gifts of knowledge have the power to culminate into innovation that results in beneficial changes. All living beings will continue to transform life as we now know it. These gifts, given to the collective consciousness of humans, exist on the grid surrounding the Earth, ready to be plucked out and developed. They will be used for the advancement of humankind in conjunction with Nature. More profound and effective information is being made available as we mature and step into the higher refinement of the light beings that we are. Whoever will sense, work with and bring these new ideas into the material plane shall be called the inventor.

As humans prove that our motivations are based on peace, more will be shown. Ideas will be given to each of us. We will collaborate with each other and Nature one step at a time, recreating a planet brimming as a constant cornucopia of abundant pure food, clean water, air and aestheticism everywhere we look. So, when a new idea floats by you, catch it and make it yours.

When You "Catch" Your Next Dream, Seek to Understand Its Ideas and Significance

The following is a simple dream that I had showing possible translations of dream symbols and metaphors:

It is Thanksgiving Day (which is a national holiday in the United States whereby the quality of gratefulness is upheld, honored and celebrated). I am entertaining others on stage in a theatrical play. I also seem to be in a dance class as a student. A man gives me flowers. Before arranging them on a table, I try to instruct the man how to become a flower anytime he wishes. I strive to teach him that in the future, whether there are physical flowers in his presence or not, by his own will, he can become a flower.

I feel that the meaning of the dream is this:

- That within all of us resides the power to learn (student).

+ Within us resides the power to teach ourselves to live with a spirit of thanksgiving each day. (Instructing on Thanksgiving.)

+ That being a performer in ways that exemplify giving thanks, and at the same time, being a student always learning how to gracefully dance through life with gratitude.

+ That each lesson, each trial we live through is just a temporary role that we are playing in the dance of life (dance class).

+ Whatever qualities those flowers represent are, even now, present and abiding within a human. It is a conscious act of will to uncover and to manifest the blossoming, the beauty, the fragrance, the joy, the tenderness, and healing sweetness of life (being like a flower). We are not to wait for someone else to make us feel this way (by his own will).

- To take an active role in existence but be not only an actor (theatrical play). Become the writer of the script also. You create your reality.

Who Among Us Has Not Awakened in the Morning Thinking, "HOW Have I Gotten Myself into This Mess?"

In life, if the metaphorical bed that you're presently lying in is cozy, curative, and to your liking, then sink in, enjoy your accomplishments and move on to the next experience. Otherwise, I say that if your bed is uncomfortable then you can remake it again differently!

In my younger years, I found myself working for other people in a beauty salon feeling increasingly under appreciated and stifled. I decided that I needed a place of my own to spread my wings and fly.

I moved forward to go into partnership with a family member in a new endeavor. Since none of the existing hotels had salons in them, I suggested we approach the biggest, newest, nicest hotel in town to find out what it would take for us to design and then rent a salon in it. Then, I was reminded by my family member that we had no money.

Regardless of our circumstances I made an appointment to meet with the hotel owners. Somehow, I just believed that this salon of my dreams could be a reality. By the time we left the meeting, we learned that the hotel owners were so thrilled with the idea of a salon going in, that they would charge us lower rent for the first several years if we built the salon ourselves. Furthermore, they also made a deal with us for the hotel to launder our many towels each day. Even with those price breaks, the rent would be towering. We left. I was bursting with excitement. My partner again reminded me that we had no money.

Next, we went to a bank. Suggesting to my partner that anything can happen and to keep our inner eyes on our goal of materializing that glorious new salon, we made a confident plea for a sizable loan. After stating that neither of us had any type of collateral, credit history, or savings to back up the kind of money we were asking for, the banker quietly stared at us. Finally, he said, "Normally, I would never grant this loan under these circumstances, however; I am retiring in two weeks if you default on this loan, I will not be here to deal with the consequences. I don't know why I'm doing this. It doesn't make sense, but I guess I just believe in you two."

The loan was granted against all odds, and the salon was a huge success. We paid back the loan in half the agreed time.

Are you ready to make your bed differently?

First, decide to make that change. You will know what situation you wish to change because it will grow increasingly more difficult to bear. You will become more uncomfortable with its pricking and nudging, preventing your peace of mind. Single this situation out. Magnify it. Define the reasons that you do not wish to have this in your life any longer. Stare at it. Ask yourself what you have done to bring this on, and why you thought you needed it. Sting yourself with honesty. Know that you have simply outgrown this old way of living, that you have learned its lessons and that it is now time to move forward.

Mentally put yourself into a more fitting and comfortable scenario. Be there. Imagine feeling the opposite of how you felt in the former unhappy situation. Feel your whole being relaxed because you innately know that this new scenario is more appropriate for you now. Pretend that you already have the situation you want. **MAKE BELIEVE** that you do. Make like you believe.

Second, begin taking the necessary steps. Keep your inner compass pointed at your goal. Each day do at least one thing toward living your new reality. Each day, take at least one step to make your vision materialize. Do not allow yourself to be discouraged. Keep your eye on your desired outcome.

Third and finally, free yourself. Repeat as needed. Don't be afraid to apply this technique to friends and lovers also.

There is no escaping the secrets of our soul. People who have had near death experiences are humans who have died for a brief period then awoke again in the same bodies that they just left. Many of these people who come back report that after they passed out of their bodies and into a spiritual realm, they began to experience the effects of their treatment of others in their most recent lifetime. They return telling us that they were made to feel, in the exact measure, any pain that they caused others. They also speak about the delight of experiencing the joy that they brought to other people's lives. We cannot hide from the secrets of our souls. What we give will eventually be given back to us.

We are not the passengers of Earth. We are the motors, the machinery that gets creation in motion. Think on this, then fill in the blank space below.

I am the most _____ on the Earth currently. Now close your eyes and feel the truth of it, taking as much time as you need.

- Enjoy the accomplishment.

- Enjoy the fullness.

- Enjoy the sensations.

- Enjoy the unshakable confidence.

Your plan has just begun its creation. Watch it unfold in its perfect timing.

Choice

We Are Each a Thread Contained in a Beautiful Tapestry

Each thread, each strand of yarn is important to hold the complete work together. When just a single thread weakens or frays, the integrity of the whole is diminished.

We have been woven together and are

responsible for our own work in maintaining the beauty and strength of the tapestry.

Therefore, let us constantly ask:

"Is what I am about to say, think, or do going to result in patching up the fabric or fray it?

Am I the razor that tears and severs, or the needle that mends?"

My tongue is a double-edged sword. Within it lies the power to create living thought forms. May my spoken words be the blade that uplifts and encourages. May my sword refrain from impaling.

Affecting the Multitudes at Large

You as seeker make a pilgrimage to others. Others make a pilgrimage to you. Each day you meet someone at work, pass on the road, touch them in dreams. One by one every encounter is an opportunity; an opportunity for mutual upliftment and exchange of energy between multitudes of people.

To Engage or Not Engage

Refraining from unflattering gossip is not just a discipline to keep our lips closed, but a natural outcome of love. For when every motivation originates from compassion, we cannot be untrue, unnecessary, or unkind.

We have learned the undesirable habit of reaction. When we react out of habit to any given situation, we give our power away. We leave ourselves vulnerable and affected by whatever circumstances or conditions that happen to be going on outside of us at the time. We are like manipulated puppets.

Imagine being in a state of mind whereby all that we think and feel comes from a state of peace. From this point, we act. We're not responding with an automatic, canned reaction.

When we choose to become peaceful, who can disturb us?

A man who was doing a two-day job in my garage began to open up and speak to me about his life. He told me that he used to have a thriving business with many employees. He said that he used to be happily married with one daughter and that they lived in a beautiful home. He went on to lament that his life took a downward turn and that he lost his business and his home and that his wife divorced him, taking their daughter.

"When did this loss of fortune occur?" I asked. He said that around three years ago, everything just started going downhill for him one thing after the other, yet he didn't know why. I asked him to think back three years. What was going on then? What happened then? After pondering about it for a moment, he brought up an incident that he remembered to be odd and eerie.

Recalling the incident, he mentioned that three years earlier, he and his wife were in a store while vacationing in New Orleans. He picked up an item that was for sale and then put it down. The store owner came up to him and asked if he was going to buy it. He said that he wasn't. She asked why. He explained that the article was too expensive. He continued shopping while the store owner followed close by. She asked him again, "Are you going to buy that item?" When he curtly answered her again that he was not, he claimed that she became angry, then looked at him straight in the eye and began speaking words in a language that he had never heard before. They left the store as quickly as they could and went on their way, he said.

I exclaimed, "She put a spell on you! She put a spell on you and you believed in it. Spells are powerless if one doesn't believe in them. You believed and allowed bad luck to come your way. Would you like to have some energy channeled toward you?" He said that he did. He sat on a chair, and I stood behind him. In a short while, his body began to shake profusely. He became very agitated and was sweating quite heavily. He started to repeat that he was going to be sick. Panting, he ran out of the open garage door and began to vomit as I watched. When it was over, he asked for water and drank it while the trembling settled down. He said that he felt much better.

He has since married a beautiful woman. He sees his daughter every other weekend. She visits in his new home, and he has opened a successful new business. His belief turned him around. He decided to trust in his own strength and invulnerability, therefore taking his power back. It was a good choice.

Trust

First Awakening Impressions

Collapsing onto my bed, I pay attention to this moment as if all is new, as if I have forgotten all that I've ever learned. I do not defend myself. I pass no judgment, but with an open heart and a blank white page in my mind, I hear. I feel. I drift into healing sleep. When I awaken, my guidance and direction are most clear. I then step more confidently into the next new, fresh moment of my life.

My Thoughts Are
in God's Mind

Can I be unworthy of my desires if it is God who along with me also desires?

Why are we endowed with innate hope and imagination if we are not meant to attain it? Does it not seem egotistical to believe that all of our ideas originate exclusively from our own minute, separate personalities?

Perhaps it is God who first plants the seeds of what we think are solely our desires. Perhaps God hopes that we will hear the whispers of our dreams, that we will not doubt, that we will believe in our worthiness.

Perhaps God's fervent hope is, "Together we can."

We learn as infants to trust and take in the nurturing sustenance given to us by our parents or caretakers. Through breast or bottle, the bond is sealed, and we are safe.

As adults, do we not have the same needs? When we hunger for direction, assistance, comfort, and assurance let us continue to suck the sweet milk at the breast of God and Mother Earth. It is the most natural thing imaginable to approach as a vulnerable, hungry child in need of sustenance and strength. This approach is necessary in order to grow and fulfill our templates, our possibilities, so that we may exemplify the splendor of who we are. This is not an action for another future time, but for now.

One form of confusion could be defined as: The willingness to be without knowing.

To say, "I don't know and it's alright," is a powerful mindset. In this state, one carries on moment by moment with an ear tuned inward and a mind focused on the situation at hand.

Being in this state becomes the elixir that

hatches previously unknown strength and creativity.

Enlightenment is not a state
that we work toward,
it is something we relax into.

Trust Nature

I used to live in a home that was located in a perfect spot for homing pigeons to roost. I noticed that there would be certain pigeons that would stand at both my front door and my back door with their little beaks nestled into the crack where the door would open. They would stand there like that for hours. The next day, those birds would be lying dead by the door.

Later on I moved to a different part of town. One day, a very large javelina was standing by my front door. That was odd because javelinas usually travel in herds or families, not alone. This javelina stood by my door and, like the pigeons, placed its' snout directly on the crack between the door and the door frame. I was happy for the company nearby, but the next morning, the javelina lay dead on its side at my front door. Do some animals want to be close to humans before death?

One evening, I was on a dinner date with a gentleman friend. After dinner, we were at my home enjoying a drink and conversation. When he left, we bid each other goodnight and I shut the door as I normally would. The next morning, I awoke to find my front door wide open and there were flying bugs everywhere. There were a lot of them! It took three weeks to rid the house of all of them. I took that happening as a sign warning me that my date from the night before was not going to be a good match for me.

In town, I used to run into a particular lady quite frequently. We always seemed to make inconsequential small talk. Finally, one day she gave me her business card and asked that I call her in order to begin a solid venture. I took her card. When I arrived home, I walked into the bathroom to find a large black widow spider against the white wall of my completely enclosed shower stall. The sight of that caused me to immediately feel that I should not pursue the business venture with the lady who gave me the card.

While having my nails done one day, I was shown a picture of a short, stocky, muscular and hairy man, due to my friends working as matchmakers. They thought the hirsute man and I would make a good couple. On my drive home, I kept thinking that I needed to buy toilet paper. A strong pull kept at me to stop and get that toilet paper, so I drove to the store and parked. Just then, my phone rang. To my surprise, it was the man whose picture was shown to me at the nail salon. He was calling for the first time to say that he wanted to set up a date for the two of us to meet. We had a short chat, and I went into the store. Once home later, I realized there was no room to place the new package because there was already plenty of toilet paper on the storage shelf. It wasn't time to purchase more toilet paper, but I did, so I was left to strategize a better storage configuration to make room for the new packages. While moving things around, I came across a can of spider repellent that I had forgotten about.

Later that evening, in the garage, I was confronted by a huge tarantula spider. "I opened the door to encourage it to go outside, but it would not. Instead, it jumped a long distance into a dark crevice. Each time I tried to capture it, he would jump into another spot, but not out the door. Clearly, he did not want to leave. Finally, it was no longer in a nook or crevice, but on the flat concrete. I quickly dropped a hollow dustpan over it with the intention of dragging the dustpan outside with the tarantula underneath to set him free. Suddenly, the dustpan flew up and was flung away by one of the tarantula's appendages! This was no ordinary spider. This guy was stocky, muscular and hairy. I remembered the can of spider repellent that I came across earlier. It would not have been apparent that it was in the house if it wasn't for the extra toilet paper that I had to find a place for earlier in the day. Would I have enough time to get that repellent can before the tarantula found a new place to hide from me? Well, now I knew just where it was and I ran, to get it. The repellent did not kill that stocky, muscular, hairy thing, but it did slow him down enough for me to finally release him back into the wild. Do you think I was being given a message?

There was a tall, but narrow flowerpot outside of my home. The top mouth of the pot was round, and the inside of the pot widened gracefully under its opening. I loved looking into the pot from my window indoors. One day, I saw several bird eggs inside of the pot, and perched on the top rim of the pot were two quail birds, the parents of the eggs. The male and female quail stood watch consistently. No one could get near the pot which held their fertilizing eggs. If anyone got too close, those birds would fly at the humans, discouraging them from getting any closer as they diligently stood watch and protected their eggs. Soon some of the eggs hatched and I looked down through the window glass to see some broken and empty eggshells. The babies hatched and left the nest. Finally, there was one egg left to hatch, and I was expecting that by the next day, the nest would be completely empty, but it wasn't. The last egg had hatched and there was one newborn baby quail running around in a circle. So adorable!

The next morning, I was awakened by loud screeching. The noise was coming from all around the entire outside of my house. Birds had surrounded and were facing my entire home and they were screeching continuously and tirelessly. I looked out the window and there were crowds of birds like I had never seen before. There were birds as far as across the street, in the trees, on the sidewalks, everywhere, and they were loud and relentless. When I looked down into the pot from my window, I could see that the last baby bird from the day before had not made it out of the pot. It was still trying to go in circles, but barely. It was moving slowly and narrowly alive. It did not have the strength to make it over the rim of the pot as the others did. Quail do not feed their young, and this newborn was badly in need of sustenance. Like a choir, all of the birds were now facing the pot, making blaring noises. Fortunately, a professional Birder happened to be close by. He arrived in front of the house. The noise that the birds were making became strikingly louder. The mother and father quail who were still sitting protectively on the rim of the pot and who earlier flew toward anyone approaching, suddenly flew away from the pot showing that they welcomed assistance. The army of birds parted creating a path to make way for the Birder to reach the little newborn. He walked up to the pot and in that moment of freeing the little one, the other birds stopped their sounds in unison. All became quiet. A reverent silence fell upon and pervaded the area. It felt like some kind of heaven. A few moments later, the birds flew away and all was back to normal. The scene was unforgettable.

I remember when I had a garden in my backyard and there were many types of flowers growing there. Each morning, I could not wait to get out of bed and take a peek at those plants. They would mirror the feelings of a person that I was involved with the day before. If that person feigned affection toward me or did not care for me truly, the flowers would be few and sparse with most falling off of the plants. Thrillingly though, if the person involved with me the day before felt sincere love for me, the flowers were copious, open and stood stronger in bloom.

Seems that there is a lot going on by my front door. There was a huge pot of white flowers growing near the door. It was so very prolific that people walking by would stop and comment on its bountifulness. My husband and I were so proud of it that he named the plant "US" in honor of the beauty of our relationship. First thing in the morning, I would go to the front window as I always did, to admire the abundance of the "US" flowers in the pot. On that morning as I set my gaze upon the pot, exactly half of the flowers stood radiantly as usual, while the other half lay down, limp and lifeless. I treated the plants with several restorative horticultural treatments. I tended to it and spoke to it and loved it, but to no avail. It just did not respond in the least. Six weeks later, my husband died. Along with him, a wall of flowers that I cultivated for his pleasure (and that he claimed were "his") all died the same day that he passed away.

Have You Ever Stopped to Think About How Special You Are?

+ God has made a commitment to you.

+ One of unconditional love.

+ Unconditional support.

+ Unconditional forgiveness.

+ God grows with you.

+ You are a necessary and unique facet of the Universe, or you wouldn't be here.

+ Your unique presence is precious and necessary to the Whole of Existence.

Are we children of the Almighty?
If we are heirs,
then we are made of the same
stuff.
All that we need already exists
within us
and without limitation.
It just takes time
and excavation of the self.

Out of Entanglement

While rolling my fingers around a knot in a gold link chain, I quietly intended Spirit to untangle it. I did not try to figure out how the knot would be undone. Instead, I just calmly rolled it between my fingers. Spirit works and the knot is undone. Just so, our lives become entangled and web-like. When asked, Spirit moves and eventually we are free once again.

Have you noticed that your relationships with loved ones and friends are rapidly changing? Are you experiencing the dropping away of people who no longer are compatible with you? Fear not for it is timely. Be glad for the lessons learned, the wisdom gained, and the space created for the new people that will now be able to enter your life. Everyone moves on to the next phase of individual learning. In the interim, maintaining steadfast trust in your relationship with yourself will carry you through the years, through the losses, the deaths, the endings and point you toward the next step.

Your fear of not wanting to be alone will compromise your essence and you may stay in a relationship that no longer thrives. I used to be afraid of being alone and have since learned that no one can hurt me when I stand strong and independent for myself. The many circumstances in my life that have forced me to be alone, out of my control, have taught me the enjoyment of trusting my own company which I have finally grown fond of and comfortable with. This is necessary in order to listen for the inkling of where to go and what to do next.

Love or fear—your choice.

Unseen Assistance

It was early morning in Western New York, and it was my turn to drive my children to school. When it was my turn to do the drive with the three, I would turn the car on and think, "Get us to their school safely, and get me back to my work, safely." I did that because I drove an old, rusty car. Some of the rust had eaten a large hole in the floor of the backseat area where the passenger's feet would normally go. I always drove this car very carefully. I dropped the little ones off and was well into my 20-minute drive to work. I was the only car in that area of the road that morning and driving at the speed limit when suddenly, I heard "boom!" I did not know where that loud sound came from until I looked into my rear-view mirror and saw my car's back rear wheel rolling down the parkway! Even though I saw that, I continued to drive on peacefully as if nothing had happened. When I got off of the parkway, the exit had a gas station waiting for me. I pulled into the station and a man came running outside toward me yelling, "This car cannot ride! This car cannot move!"

I told him what happened. He pointed to the missing wheel and excitedly explained that when the wheel came off, the car should have immediately stopped and tipped. He was incredulous and kept saying that it was impossible for my car to have driven normally on three wheels all that way. Exuding internal gratitude, I reminded him that he just watched me roll into his gas station.

Walking a White Path Alone

While in my late twenties, a beautiful young girl who was a friend and a worker in my beauty salon approached me troubled. She had begun what we now know as channeling, but did not understand what was happening to her. She revealed that she began to feel impelled to gather a pen and a notebook. Holding the pen, her hand began to move automatically as page after page, she formed large spirals. With each page turned, the spirals progressively looked a little smaller and a little tighter, until gradually there were copious amounts of tiny spirals all over the pages. To her surprise, the spirals began to turn into script. By the time she reached the last pages of the notebook, actual words were forming. Her spirit guide introduced himself to her through the written words on the pages. Eventually, writing evolved into speaking and so began her channeling.

During a session with my friend and her guide, I was given a spiritual health check-up. It began with an energetic feeling that started at the top of my head and slowly made its way down, scanning the length of my body down to my feet. A few moments later, her guide reported that I had a minor disorder in a particular part of my inner body that I had been unaware of. Upon getting an X-ray, her guide had been correct.

Another time, I asked her guide to speak to me about my soul's purpose. He said, "You walk a white path alone." I did not like hearing his statement, especially during that young time of my life when the mere thought of being alone was deeply disturbing. It was not my plan, and I tried to avoid it.

Over time, however, life has honed me and

involuntarily forced aloneness upon me. One by one, circumstances happen, and people drop away. I find myself thinking, acting, understanding and expecting in ways that are unlike other people. Such differences require a degree of isolation, and to my surprise, at this point, aloneness comes as somewhat of a relief.

One learns to "hear" the voice of intuition, until maybe for the first time, one trusts oneself. The need for outside validation dissipates, eventually realizing that I was not meant to fit into expectations, but instead, to be unique.

It takes courage, Dear Ones, conviction and faith to finally realize that separateness is not necessarily loneliness. I realize now that I am never without divine urges that point toward the next direction, which might mean just staying still for a while. I have come to understand that it is enough to simply be, as a lighthouse in the dark, holding light on the planet for others that they may find their way. Yes, I walk a white path physically alone, but I now walk feeling the constant accompaniment of benevolence and protection.

Decide to Know

Since we lived on opposite sides of the country, I visualized that when it was time for my father to pass away, I would somehow be shown in advance whether through a dream or by any type of intuition. I needed to know when to travel across the country in time to be with him when he crossed over. When I began to hear song lyrics in my mind telling me that my father's life here was growing short, I knew that it was time to travel to him. On my way to the airport, I remember telling others, "My father is going to die." When I arrived at his residence asking about his condition, I was told that he was strong, well, and expected to live a long time yet. During dinner we spoke. I told him that if he was not ready to pass over, then the two of us would have a wonderful visit, but if he was ready to go, then I had come to hold his hand. I reminded him of the times in my life when I was afraid, and he was there to hold my hand. Now, it was my turn.

After dinner, instead of his usual routine of looking out the window, and then watching TV, he decided to go to bed. From that moment on, he did not want to eat or drink anymore. He stopped speaking. Instead, he allowed me to talk. I spoke of how he unassumingly affected and assisted others. I told him that of all the things I had learned in this lifetime of most value was all taught by his wordless examples, and I told him about how the stone fireplaces and brick walls that he built would stand as a testament to his art. I sang the songs that he loved and told him the jokes that he used to love to tell. For three precious days, I held his hand. Toward the end, something that I could not see, but must have been delightful was drawing his attention to the corner of the room. I watched the joy on his handsome face and how his soulful eyes smiled. Something wonderful was waiting for him.

Your Legacy and Posterity

*If, at the end of life, we consider
all that we have given and received,
and can smile contentedly,
we are the wealthiest of all.*

- The act of peeling an apple brings one closer to its core or its beginning.

- The apple is a reflection of its seed.

- The seed is a reflection of the apple.

- Peeling away the layers of my ego, I get closer to my own core, the very substance of me.

- My life mirrors my soul, and my soul is a reflection of my life.

---

*How extensively we have
loved is the lamp that
lights the way for others.*

One morning, I was greeted by this note that was lying on the dining room table for me. It was written by one of my daughters, Tara, who was then eight years old, and my seven-year-old son, Anthony (Che Che), who collaborated.

This is their letter that they left for me exhibiting the practical aspects of their being:

Dear Mother,
We love you very much! You could just die like snap! If you die we'll freak out! We love you a lot!

Here is a poem:
Roses are Read Violets are Blue
Tara Loves Mamma Anthony Too!!

By: Tara & Anthony or Che Che
We Love You!
P.S. Can I have your shoes when you die?

The Juicy Fruit of My Labor Awaits Me

Is it true that when I leave my body to once again transition, that I will be able to receive whatsoever I have given away while on Earth? Am I to meet the conscience of my personal self, who once occupied a human body? If this is true, then I wish to experience the most graceful, sublime and wondrous of gifts. Therefore, I shall live my life giving away the attributes of those I will later embrace. Oh, I want kindness! When someone sincerely seeks knowledge that I possess, I become the teacher. I like to leave things better than I found them. The frequent wishes that I invoke upon myself, and every human are large and lenient. The origins of the blessings that I bestow are pure, sincere and lovely. Oh, I want kindness!

I Will Get That
Which I Have Given

There was a woman who could not seem to control her nymphomania. She would go to military bases and have sexual relations with all manner of men, even those unfamiliar to her. She knew that her lifestyle was unsafe and wanted to understand why she was so strongly driven toward excessive sex and could not get gratification. The woman sought out Edgar Cayce, a renowned psychic who did a past life reading on her. During her reading, Cayce spoke about another lifetime, where she was a woman of the cloth, a nun, in charge of overseeing rehabilitation patients. In that lifetime, she had no tolerance or empathy for others and especially those with addictions. She caused her patients to feel guilt and unworthiness. She was in a position to help those people, but instead, she hindered them with her intolerance and judgment. "In this lifetime," Cayce said, "You meet yourself." He told her that in another lifetime she had no tolerance for addiction, especially those with sexual addiction. She then understood that she must learn what it is like not only to have an addiction, but to experience the addiction that she judged others for most harshly.

In another case, there was a man who had a strong desire to be a father. For years, his wife had much difficulty getting pregnant and then there were miscarriages. When they finally did succeed in having a child, the husband was completely overjoyed, but within months, the baby died of sudden infant death syndrome. In deep despair, the man went to Edgar Cayce for a reading in hope of understanding why this had happened. During the trance, Cayce spoke of another lifetime where the man was the father of five children who loved and needed him. The children longed for his attention and affection, however; he didn't care for them. Through Cayce's reading, it was explained that in this lifetime, he must experience the longing for the love of a child but not have it. Cayce also revealed that the soul of his baby was aware of the upcoming crib death it would experience yet chose to be born despite it. The baby knew its father had to experience what he had done to someone else in another lifetime before the father could be free. The baby loved the father so much that he came in for a short duration so that the father could live out the pain that he had coming to him. Once learned, the father's debt was paid, freeing him again. The slate was wiped clean.

Me First Honoring Self

Beauty of its own nature stops us momentarily, engages us, and imparts its gifts. We are left with an incentive to aspire. We are left inspired. We are softened.

Beauty is its own meditation and pulls out of humanity the innate yearning for peace.

It resides everywhere. We may find it in humility, talent, understanding, deep laughter, faith, tolerance, a smile, truth, integrity, wisdom, the life in a pair of eyes, unadulterated generosity, and love shaped into form.

Allow the world to gaze upon your loveliness. Be not haughty, but gracious in others' appreciation of you. To be conceited over one's beauty is a dichotomy, for conceit is of the personality. Beauty's origin is the soul.

Everyone possesses beauty somewhere. Whatever is beautiful about you, within you— find it, cherish it as your reward for lovely deeds done long ago. You have earned your beauty.

True Education

If the same problems seem to recur in your life, and you'd like to end the cycle, try a different, more compassionate approach to handling them.

Be compassionate with yourself and your truths foremost, and then to the problem at hand.

When the same types of problems seem to appear in your life, gently allow yourself to reflect and take notice of what it is that you are being called to change. Ask, "What lesson am I to discover here? What have I not yet learned through these tough experiences?"

Once you allow light to be shed on the answer to what you are to learn and then permit yourself to act on that knowledge, you will no longer have to live through those similar themes of problems that plagued you earlier. The lesson will have been grasped.

School is out.

Every human is imbued with a unique quality that is characteristic to that person alone. Without fail, there is at least one ability that each human being possesses that is unlike any other. That distinctive gift can only be given to the world by that individual.

What is your unique ability that only
you alone can contribute to the world?
Name it.
Know your gift.

Find Time to Lose Time

There are activities that, when fully entered into, cause us to lose track of time.

Bring to mind at least one, whereby you have become so focused that time seems non-existent. You know the feeling.

It is during these moments that we are infused with the power of peace, the power to heal, to love, to transform, and to understand.

A Redwood in a Forest . . .

*Is it any less a tree if no one
singles out its beauty?*

*Is it any less a tree if it is not
used for shade or paper or fire?*

*Its branches sway in the
wind, it does not break.*

*With or without worldly
recognition, it is unobtrusively
content to be what it is:
strong, solid, unique, consummate, silent.*

*May I learn to be content like
the Redwood.*

My only plan to be in good standing with my soul, at least in this lifetime here on Earth, is to always be aware of never acting in a way that will make my conscience ache. From birth, I have always longed to experience "more God" in my life. I wanted to feel assured of the presence of whatever or whomever created me. Many nights, I would sit on my bedroom windowsill looking into the night sky. The sound of Niagara Falls at night, just 13 blocks from our home, was loud and mesmerizing.

I pondered the important questions that as a child, no one spoke about. "Truly, where have I come from? What is to become of me? Where will I ultimately go? How do I fit into this galaxy?" I wanted to understand, and I wished to be in control of my existence. I wanted to know that my life mattered. I wondered where I would find the answers.

Growing up, I was raised in strict religious schools and taught to participate in their traditional sacred practices. I joined extra-curricular church activities, hoping that all the diligent effort, prayers, rituals, and sacrifices would somehow bring me into some type of tangible relationship with the Divine. I was dutiful and always tried to do better, but still, the close relationship that I longed to feel with my Maker was absent. Time passed. After so many years of disillusion, my children and I set out looking to expand our search for a spiritual home. We went to all types of organizations that worshiped in temples, cathedrals, and synagogues. Much was said and much was shown, but a spiritual home we did not find. After all of that, here are some of the things that I have learned:

+ The evilest entity that I have encountered has been within religious organizations.

+ My relationship to the Divine has nothing to do with religion or learning rituals.

+ I have freed myself to find the sacred in everything and everyone, if I allow myself to look deeply and intently enough, I find it.

- The only measure that I live by now is to be sure that I am treating others as I wish to be treated. In this way, I do no harm, feel no guilt and my conscience is always clean.

Relax Yourself.
Get Away from Unrelenting Worries by:

- Closing your eyes and bringing all of your attention to the blank screen at the top of your nose.

- Listening to the music of nature; rain or wind or crickets . . .

- Just droping everything and doing something that you like and that pleases you.

If you ever find yourself feeling jealous, affirm over and over until you feel the truth of this statement:

"I am enough.
I am more than enough
and I know that everything is always
working out for the best for me."

Then sit back and enjoy the scenario.

Because of his worthwhile help to me, I once asked an esteemed advisor what I could do for him. He replied, "Begin to give yourself the peace and sense of well-being that you give to others. That would do me well." His eloquent answer stirred something deep inside of me. I knew him to be an unselfish being, and yet he was urging me to be indulgent with myself.

I later learned to give myself permission to relax so that I might fill myself up first with whatever it is that I deem necessary.

I learned that one must take care of one's own

needs, whether they be on the level of healing, loving, pursuing activities of interest, sexuality, or free time.

That each person seeks joy in a unique way and that he is to allow himself that joy.

Instead of concentrating only on giving to the other, a person must value himself enough to focus first on his own important requirements.

That the overflow of fullness spreads.

What a delightful surprise to find that once one is satisfied, giving becomes almost effortless. Giving is simply the extra pleasure that spills from one who is already full. In this state of contentment, it becomes unnecessary to mentally "send out" positive thoughts to another. Your overflow will automatically spill onto others and the world.

There is nothing to do. Only to be. Let us together, have the courage to live happily ever after. Go forth, my fellow travelers. Like the sun, shine on us all. Shine!

Dreams

Once I had a dream. In it, the skillful, massive, protective hands of the Divine held an artichoke as if it were the rarest of treasures.

These hands began patiently and with the utmost reverence, to pluck one by one, the leaves of the artichoke. First, the tough, coarse leaves of the exterior were taken. By and by, the more tender leaves of the inner layers began to reveal themselves. Steadfastly but without haste, the fingers worked, intent on reaching the center.

Then finally, the purpose was accomplished. Holding it as one would a newborn child taking its first breath of life, these hands marveled at the magnitude and worth of the heart.

I cannot help but think how much we are like artichokes.

Our Dreams Are Personal Counseling Sessions from Mother Nature

I awaken with the following dream message flowing through my mind:

"Follow the sun. If you give it all you've got, you can do it."

I interpreted this to mean: Move toward and become that light which heals, nurtures, and lifts spirits. More importantly, remember that the sun does not choose where it will shine, but unabashedly sheds its light equally on all creatures.

Become like the sun.

At the time that this dream occurred, I had no idea of the prophetic implications involved. Many years after having this dream, I discovered and began the practice of solar healing through sun gazing, which was to begin an important and meaningful phase of my life.

Understanding the self through recording one's dreams, interpreting them correctly, and applying the knowledge gained from man's nocturnal adventures can be a main vehicle to both spiritual growth and success in everyday life. Simple to follow, yet invaluable methods are available to decode dream symbols, therefore, unlocking the doorway to the subconscious and beyond.

All humans sleep and all humans dream. It is an established fact that dreams are a significant contributing factor to our physical and mental health. People experiment with drugs, alcohol, and biofeedback in hopes of exploring the inner realms of the human psyche, and to experiment with consciousness expansion. Because dreams are commonplace, many people belittle the importance of them, but working with dreams can be compared to having one's own personal therapist or guru who visits freely each evening. Western man has relied so heavily on the conscious mind, that he has forgotten the knowledge that life can be greatly transformed by the unconscious. The pendulum is beginning to swing back though, bringing with it a rebirth of interest in the dream world and its' benefits. Self-analysis through dreams has proven to be an invaluable tool for the person on the path of self-improvement.

Dreams come to assist in some of the following ways:

1. To face, accept, and finally understand oneself and others

2. To give practical guidance concerning one's life work

3. To offer information concerning the healing of emotional, spiritual, or physical health problems

4. To stimulate creativity

5. To increase serenity and inner peace

6. To stimulate memories of past lives or out of body experiences

7. To develop a stronger connection to the spiritual nature

8. To expand the consciousness

9. To encourage and inspire

Edgar Cayce, one of the truly remarkable psychics of all time, felt that all visions and dreams are given for the benefit of the individual, if he would but interpret them correctly. He believed that dreams are the activities in the unseen world of the real self.

Visions or dreams, in whatever character they may come, are the reflection of three levels:

1. The physical or conscious mind

2. The mental or subconscious mind

3. The spiritual or superconscious mind

Most dreams originate from one of these three levels, although it is not uncommon for them to overlap.

Dreams originating from the physical level deal with physiological needs such as sexual release, or perhaps suggestions concerning foods, medication or exercise that the dreamer may require, etc., and are therefore useful. Other dreams from the physical level are often meaningless in that they are merely responses to bad food combinations, overindulgence in food (or the spices in food), drugs, alcohol, illness, fatigue or disinterest. All may cause distorted information.

It is common to dream of a phone ringing as a substitute for a real-life alarm clock, or to dream of snow, and awaken realizing that one is physically cold. Many dreams from the physical level are simply a rehash of the day's activities. For instance, after having spent the day toiling through dirty laundry and housecleaning, a person might dream of climbing a mountain of soiled clothes. Someone who was overtaxed that day with paperwork, might dream of being "rained on" by paper and trying to run for cover. These dreams are samples of a carryover of the day's activities and often do not require any further interpretation.

The majority of dreams are initiated by the mental, subconscious level, and cover a wider range of experience. Dreams utilize humor, proper names or sometimes use a play on words, to get a point across. A play on words is used in the following example:

A woman is going through the experience of being raped in her dream. She later finds in her waking life that her business partner was embezzling and taking large sums of money that personally hurt her.

Another woman asked for guidance concerning a first romantic date that she was to go on the following day with a new gentleman in her life. Upon awakening, she heard continually, the proper name of "Chevy Chase, Chevy Chase . . ." being repeated over and over. The next evening, her date drove her to a secluded parking area and tried to forcibly seduce her. As she glanced at the car's dashboard, she saw the word CHEVY and realized that her dream of the night before was forewarning her of a "Chevy Chase." Double meanings of words should be watched for, such as dreaming of an American nickel could represent the "five senses," or to dream of fire could mean getting "fired" from a job.

The information received from visions does not tell the dreamer what to do, but rather informs the dreamer, leaving one free to accept or reject. One man dreamed of drowning in a pool of alcohol. The dream didn't say, "Stop drinking!" but certainly paints a vivid picture of the direction in which the dreamer is going. It has been said that one picture is worth a thousand words.

Many problems in life are derived from a lack of awareness. Self-revealing dreams will focus on that lack, but the dreamer should not be frightened by them because dreams come to help, not hinder. In other words, no one will be given more than he or she is able to deal with at any given time. What is termed a nightmare usually occurs because the dreamer needs to be reminded of a problem that he or she is not solving, or an issue that has been suppressed. Stressful dreams in which the body is in difficulty should be paid close attention to because the subconscious can sense an illness long before any physical symptoms appear.

If the dreamer is out of balance or takes any act, attitude or emotion too far, the subconscious will call for compensatory readjustment or self-regulation. For instance, a person who dreams of laughing has probably been taking life too seriously. To dream of being a nun could denote that the dreamer may have been placing too much emphasis on sex, or that the dreamer may be in need of more quiet, secluded time.

Some dreams defy explanation and might be termed as telepathy, clairvoyance or can be actual experiences of other realities. Sometimes, the setting in a dream where the action takes place in other time frames, or where the characters in the dream are wearing costumes from the far past, could be indications of past life experiences the dreamer may have lived. These dreams warn the dreamer against repeating the same old mistakes or explain the dreamer's reactions to certain people or places.

Prophetic dreams occur as an aid to help the dreamer handle an upcoming situation. One man had recurring dreams of his son being arrested and going to prison. A month later, when this actually took place, the man was prepared to handle it emotionally because he had already "lived it" in his dream life.

During World War I, Hitler had a dream in which he saw himself buried by an avalanche of earth and hot iron. When he awoke, he left his position only to find that moments later, an explosion had occurred where he had been sleeping and buried his companions alive.

A well-known prophetic dream belonged to

Abraham Lincoln in which he saw his own coffin just a few days before his death.

The Bible is a plethora of many prophetic dreams, especially the Book of Revelation, which is a compilation of John's own dreams and visions.

Sometimes dreams are literal. One man dreamed that a person in a white laboratory coat appeared to him and said, "Play the lottery today. The numbers are 6839." The man did as he was told, and those numbers came in that day.

Another person's messages were given to her in the form of music and song. Upon awakening, she would hear a song playing in her mind. After scrutinizing the words in the song, she knew that she had received clear guidance through those words on an issue that she had been concerned about before retiring.

A woman who started to seek spiritual assistance in her life began receiving profound guidance in her dreams and also began to experience a loving presence around her. Before going to sleep, she asked that this benevolent presence communicate to her in a more direct way. That evening, she experienced a musical dream wherein a woman and an invisible man were singing to one another. (The music and lyrics were from Andrew Lloyd Weber with the exception of one word that was changed. In the dream, the word MUSIC was replaced by the word BEAUTY.) Since the woman was an artist, decorator and hair stylist, her life's work was to bring beauty into the world. This change of the word MUSIC to BEAUTY, reflected in the dreamer a deeper meaning in that she felt convinced of being assisted in her creativity by acknowledging life in the spiritual realms. In the dream, a woman sings these words:

"Father once spoke of an angel.
I used to dream he'd appear.
Now as I dream, I can sense him
and I know he's here.
Angel of Beauty, guide and guardian
come to me."

An invisible man responds to her, also sing-ing:

> *"Flattering child, you shall know me.*
> *See why in shadow I hide.*
> *Look at your face in the mirror.*
> *I am there inside.*
> *I am your Angel . . . "*

These dreams emanating from the spiritual level have the most transformative effect. They leave one with a feeling of peace, wholeness and are seldom forgotten. They offer encouragement, inspiration and insights into the meaning of life. The desire and conscious effort to live a beautiful, inspiring lifestyle, and daily meditation have proven to be powerful tools to connect with the higher realms of consciousness and encourage more dreams from the spiritual level.

If a dream doesn't have a literal meaning, it will utilize symbols or metaphors as a means of communication since the subconscious does not have the use of verbal language. Conventional symbols such as a heart, the sun, a flower, fire, etc., are understood and their meanings are generally accepted and agreed upon by most. However; their meaning would take on a different significance if there was a personal association with it. For example, the symbol of rain in a dream would take on a different meaning for a farmer than it would for people in other professions.

Carl Jung proved his suspicion that the meaning of certain symbols is the same for everyone. He termed these symbols "archetypes" or universal symbols. People in the African jungle who lived thousands of miles away from other humans, with no means of communication to society, used symbols that are identical to people living in other parts of the world. There is something deep within our subconscious that causes all of us to react in the same way to these symbols although we are not consciously aware of their meaning. Some examples of archetypal symbols are a circle, a crescent, a star, etc. Many fairy tales contain these symbols that everyone seems to understand. Think of the symbol of a seed or a wolf's teeth. Most people get a general feeling of the universal meaning of these archetypal symbols.

Whether or not one's dreams are recalled,

everyone dreams four or five times per night at approximately ninety-minute intervals. If at first one isn't successful at recalling and analyzing the dream state, the following suggestions could be considered:

1. Think, talk and read about dreams. Join a dream study group. (The Senoi and Mayan Indians encourage all their children under the age of twelve, to talk about their dreams over breakfast, a most meaningful tradition! They believe that therapeutic benefits are derived from simply listening about their children's dreams. As long as they followed this practice, crimes of violence were nonexistent within the tribes.)

2. Be open to change.

3. Suggest to yourself each evening before sleep, that you will remember your dreams upon awakening. If this is not accomplished immediately, do not worry. Success will come with consistent attempts.

4. Convince your subconscious of your sincerity by keeping a pen, notebook or voice recorder, and an easy light source such as a flashlight or touch lamp close at hand while sleeping. Decide to maintain a daily dream journal and record your dreams immediately upon awakening. Do this prior to performing any physical functions such as using the bathroom or answering a phone.

5. Program your dreams. If you wish for a symbolic comment concerning a particular area of your life, or maybe you would desire to spend more time in the spiritual levels, then instruct yourself to do so. Decide that you will be shown information on the subject that you inquire about.

6. Work on analyzing your dreams every day, so that dream progression can be seen.

7. If you're unable to interpret the meaning of a dream that you have received, suggest to yourself the following evening that the

message repeat itself in more clearly understood symbols.

8. Some nightmares which bring with them an inability to move or to cry out can sometimes be an indication of eating the wrong diet. When the offending foods are singled out and the diet is changed, these nightmares usually end. Most recurring nightmares, however, come to get our attention in a progressively, stronger manner because the dreamer hasn't listened to and taken heed from prior guidance. Once the message of the nightmare is understood and the dreamer makes the necessary changes according to the guidance given the nightmare will cease.

9. If dreams are unchanged over the years, this might be an indication of the dreamer's resistance to change.

10. Dreams of ill health can represent either literal or symbolic warnings.

11. Many times, dreams present an opportunity to connect with those who have passed on. These may be valid encounters of bodiless consciousness communicating.

12. Most dreams are primarily about oneself. Fewer dreams relate to family, friends or world events.

13. Be consistent. Persistence is necessary in familiarizing yourself with the symbolic, feeling language of dreams.

14. Daily prayer, meditation, and maintaining a seeking attitude all improve the quality and reception of dreams.

The first step in determining the meaning of a dream is to consider a possible literal meaning such as warnings or reminders before moving on to metaphorical interpretations. If there is a metaphor, then take the appropriate action.

One woman dreamed that her fiancé's former girlfriend unexpectedly came into town to visit her former boyfriend, the dreamer's future husband. She dreamed of the two of them making love, and of her fiancé's true desire to marry his former girlfriend. Upon confronting him the next day, she learned that the contents of her dream were indeed, actually happening at the same time that she had the dream.

I once dreamed of being caught and arrested for sales and possession of an illegal substance. In the dream, I found myself in the back of a police van, afraid because I was being taken to jail. In my conscious everyday life, I was aware that the dream had a literal meaning, not for me, but for someone I knew. I warned that person to be careful and to consider that the dream content could be a probability and to be aware of what he was doing and the possible consequences. A very short time later, the person was arrested and sent to prison. (In retrospect, perhaps I should not have conveyed the precognitive literal dream to him because he accused me of lying about the fact that I had a dream and instead, wrongly believed that I went to the police earlier and set him up to be arrested. I was blamed.)

Do not always assume that the literal message is the only meaning. If the dream makes no sense when taken literally, then it should be viewed as a metaphorical statement of something in the dreamer's life. There can be many levels of meaning.

One man dreamed of picking and eating an abundance of beautifully, ripe fruit on a bright, sunny day. The literal meaning was a suggestion to consume more fresh fruit, since the man's diet had been deficient lately, causing him to be constipated. Looking at the metaphorical meaning of the same dream, this man had recently begun a new business venture, and was unsure of whether the enterprise could sustain him financially. The symbolic interpretation revealed that soon he would reap the "fruits" of his labor, and that things would turn out "bright and sunny."

Prepare for your dream life adventure. You may wish to ask your higher self to assist you to awaken from sleep with a comment or understanding on a particular subject. Write down your dream immediately upon awakening. As you work to unravel the meaning, take notes, write them down in a notebook. If the dream is not a literal one or does not utilize wordplay, the following suggestions are recommended to discover the underlying meaning:

1. Date your dreams so that you can find a relationship between them and the events in your life. You will find that your dreams are both proactive and retroactive.

2. Be objective. Stand back and view the dream as if it were a film, or as if reading a magazine article. Ask yourself, "If this dream was a movie, how would I summarize in one sentence, its' basic contents? If my dream was a magazine article, and I was asked to write a heading for it, what would that heading be? What is the ACTION of this dream?" (Emphasize the action, not the actors.)

3. Note the summary, the heading or the action of the dream. With these in mind, ask, "Where in my life is this action, etc., taking place?"

4. Ask, "In an ideal situation, what would this dream want?"

5. Re-experience the emotions and the feeling tone of the dream. Ask, "What relationship do these emotions have to the present conditions in my life?"

6. Analyze the symbols. Isolate each dream character and each significant object in the dream. Study each. Become in your mind, the character or object that you are focusing on. What characteristics does it have? What are its' qualities? What does it do? How does it work? Find the personal associations that the symbols have for you. Remember, there is no right or wrong meaning for any symbol.

To dream of snow would indicate a different meaning for an individual involved in a new romance, (possibly predicting a cold nature), than it would for another who might be working in the home heating business. ("Snow", in this case could be predicting an upcoming cold spell or a busy season.)

Dreamwork uncovers practical guidance that alters existing behavior patterns, emotions and attitudes, therefore aiding in the transformation of the lower materialistic nature of man, to a higher more spiritual one. The final and most critical step is ACTING on the information gleaned. One day at a time, as you apply what you learn and feel from your dream message, then the next step will be shown. You will know the next action to take and the next personal experience for you will unfold.

The true meaning of a dream is not only understanding the message conveyed within it, but what we then do with that knowledge. Act on it. If, at first, the message is unclear as to the interpretation of a dream, do not worry. Another will follow, usually involving the same theme. Upon examining two of these dreams together, one will discover that a pattern or theme begins to emerge revealing a preoccupation or progression of a situation in one's life.

The same theme may occur with the same dreamer while having a different meaning each time, depending on the person's circumstances at the time of each dream. A dream is correctly interpreted only when it makes sense to you in terms of your present life and moves you to positive change. A dream is incorrectly deciphered if the interpretation leaves you unmoved and disappointed. Dreams come to expand, not diminish you.

The following are six of the most common dream themes and their general meanings:

1. Falling—If there is no literal warning message, then look for the metaphorical "fall" such as entertaining feelings of guilt or "falling from grace," "falling back," "falling short," "falling in love," fear of failure or lack of a solid foundation.

2. Nudity—Feeling exposed, vulnerable, open to criticism, free from constriction or undisguised; "naked truth," "bearing it all."

3. Flying—Rising above a situation, astral projection, a desire to be free, "flying high," or being "up in the air" about a problem or decision.

4. Taking an Examination—Being tested on some level either literally, physically or

spiritually being "put to the test," "examine the situation."

5. Losing or Finding Valuables—Literal meanings, a "loss of the moral way or finding of the moral way," gaining or detaching from things we've "valued."

6. Sexual Dreams—A oneness, an integration of two ideas or attitudes such as male/female principles, wisdom/love, intellect/intuition, wish fulfillment, being excited, "turned on" or "embracing" an activity in life, "taking into ourselves" that which excites us. The "libido" one extends to a particular area of life. (During REM, rapid eye movement of sleep, the sexual organs become excited, irrespective of dream content.)

Experiments in what is called "dream incubation," are being done with notable results. In one study, a group of people all unfamiliar with one another agreed to dream for one of the participants named Pat. Pat asked that the group's dreams target a specific area of his personal life. The following day, each member of the group reported his or her first impressions upon awakening that morning. After listening to the group's dreams and discussing possible interpretations, Pat was informed for the first time of his estranged brother's illness and impending death. (Pat had never forgiven his brother for past transgressions that left deep wounds that he had incurred by his brother's behavior. Therefore, Pat had built a strong emotional wall between them.) Through the discussion, Pat discovered that his estranged brother sincerely wanted his forgiveness before he died. Pat left the group with a conviction to act on the messages of the dreamers. It seems that monitored dreaming in groups contains the possibility of unlimited potential for information and insight.

The author Elsie Sechrist eloquently wrote, "To the disbelieving, dreams may simply be a puzzling, disturbing or totally irrelevant phenomena. To the individual who desires self-improvement and communication with his divine self, dreams will show the way. To the dedicated person who seeks to serve his fellow man and God, dreams will bring understanding, joy and peace of mind, for they are the Magic Mirror of the soul."

Synopsis

The same powerful inspiration that came to me in my earlier years remains, truly, to be the one basic tenet that continues to comprehensively guide my life, and that is to behave toward others as I want others to behave toward me, wishing upon all beings that which I want for myself.

I am you.
You are me.
We are one.

Last year, I spoke last year's language.
Another voice, a different voice appropriate
to tomorrow will render next year's words.
Take comfort, loved ones, knowing that
to reach an end is to make a beginning.

Bibliography

Sechrist, Elsie with Edgar Cayce. *Dreams Your Magic Mirror.* New York: Warner Books, 1974.

Recommended Readings

Books

- *Agartha: Journey to the Stars* by Meredith Lady Young

- *Living With Joy* by Sanaya Roman and Duane Packer

- *Dream Dictionary* by Tony Crisp

Website

- www.solarhealing.com (Hira Ratan Manek, HRM)

- www.oceanalchemy.com (Master Alchemist and trusted ORMUS maker, Don Nance)

- www.ormustech.com (Master Alchemist and trusted ORMUS maker, William Bull)

- www.subtleenergies.com

*While ORMUS or (Orbitally Rearranged Mono-atomic Elements or ORMes) has many varied advantages, there is one interesting benefit that I have discovered. Ingesting certain types of ORMUS may result in experiencing some of the same results as sun gazing although less intense.

Videos

- The Heyoka Kryon

- Kryon Late Night Series

- Kryon with Lee Carroll

- Binaural Beats

- Rife Frequencies

www.ingramcontent.com/pod-product-compliance
Lightning Source LLC
Chambersburg PA
CBHW021617120626
46545CB00001B/273